Table of Cont

Introduction

Congratulations on purchasing *Introducing Psychology,* and thank you for doing so.

Have you ever wondered why people do what they do? Or what makes you think or act the way you do? Usually, people pride themselves as being particularly unique. We assume that we are entirely autonomous, able to make decisions on what we want, and need with ease. We assume that there is no way that someone else can control our actions or feelings simply because we are superior beings and entirely rational.

However, people tend to forget that, at the root, they are not as powerful as they try to make themselves out to be. Our methods of thinking are not unique in any sense—in fact, the thinking of other people can be regularly and readily predicted by those who study it. In particular, everything that you do reduces down to a certain triggering of neural impulses via brain chemistry. That feeling of falling in love is nothing but hormones and electrical impulses, as is the anger that you feel when someone wrongs you, and the joy that you feel when you are finally able to hold your newborn child for the first time. Effectively, everything is able to be reduced down to simple numbers. Just as the computer processes all of its functions in impulses, so too does the brain.

Psychology seeks to understand the why and how of what happens in the mind. In particular, it is the scientific study of the mind. Of course, there are different interpretations of what that could mean. It could be the understanding of what the mind does and seeing exactly how, on a biological level, it works. It could be watching to understand the behaviors themselves. Ultimately, what is important in psychology is figuring out exactly what is going on within the human mind in order to understand how it functions and how to predict behaviors.

Understanding psychology can help you better understand people themselves. When you know the reasons why people get attached, how these attachments occur, and how to facilitate that sort of attachment, you can very effectively understand how to work around them. If you know that certain things will get certain reactions, you can ensure that you always get the best reactions from those that you interact with.

Within this book, you will be introduced to entry-level psychology. You will get an idea of the history of psychology and how it has changed over time with advancements in technology and what people can do. You will see how there are several perspectives through which you can address behaviors and actions as well. You will see how psychology impacts every aspect of your life, looking in-depth at emotional intelligence and psychology, the emotional state of someone else and psychology, and more. You will gain a solid understanding of what emotions are, how they are believed to occur, and why we have them. You will learn about the seven universal emotions and what they are meant to convey. You will learn about managing those very emotions, as well as any thoughts that may underlie them in an art known as cognitive behavioral therapy, which is used in order to combat mental health issues such as anxiety or anger. You will then be guided through three distinct concepts: How psychology impacts your relationship, your chances at success, and how it can ward off procrastination. When you understand these concepts, you can then begin to take action, taking advantage of your newfound knowledge of how the mind works in order to ensure that you are able to do always put your best foot forward. You can use your knowledge of how your mind works to benefit your relationships, help yourself move toward success, and to fight procrastination.

There are plenty of books on this subject on the market, thanks again for choosing this one! Every effort was made to ensure it is full of as much useful information as possible; please enjoy!

Chapter 1: A Brief History of Psychology

For as long as people have been able to record history, they have been interested in understanding the mind. People have been interested in the study of behavior and how the mind works even in ancient Greece. This is significant—people have been trying to figure out how people work and why they work the way that they do for as long as they have been recording.

Of course, in the ancient days, the explanations were often filled with spells and exorcisms that were designed to drive away the demons that were assumed to be the root cause. What is significant about this is the fact that it began the look at the human mind, creating a clearly defined point between what is considered normal behaviors versus what would be considered to be a problematic sort of behavior that people reject. It was known that certain patterns of behaviors were problematic and not within the realm of normalcy—the people seeking to understand how to treat these abnormal behavioral patterns were engaging in a sort of primitive psychology.

The history of psychology has come a long way from believing that people with abnormal behavior are possessed and require some sort of exorcising in order to treat them. Nowadays, people's proverbial demons are able to be addressed and treated through other means, such as with medication and therapeutic processes, to ensure that people get what they need in order to thrive.

Within this chapter, we will see a comparison of then and now, as well as looking at key moments in between. Understanding the evolution of how this information was discovered and why it has worked the way that it does is critical to better understanding people in general. We will see how what was once the philosophy of the mind and thought eventually shifted over into modern psychology that is actionable.

Keep in mind that, as you read this, you are getting a condensed timeline of some of the most notable moment in psychology. There is more to it than just what is presented to you, but in order to avoid writing a book of its own, you will be provided just the gist of what happened within each of the steps from ancient psychology all the way to modern cognitivism.

Ancient Psychological Thought

Even in ancient history, there was a need to understand the mind, the brain, and the workings of humankind. In fact, some of the first medical recordings in history will relate to the brain and behavior. People sought to understand how not only the body worked, but how to heal it as well. Around the world, it is possible to find all sorts of documentation on how psychology has developed, from Egypt to China, and from Greece to India.

The Edwin Smith Papyrus

Perhaps the most ancient known acknowledgment of the brain and how it worked is found in the Edwin Smith Papyrus. Named for the individual that bought it in the 1800s, this scroll is believed to date back to around 1600 BCE. In particular, this scroll described details on actively treating several different medical conditions and injuries that are important to understand. These not only include injuries and attempts to treat ailments such as a gaping wound, but also information about the brain, the nerves, and how the injuries of certain types can create certain unintended side effects.

In particular, it was discussed that brain injuries would impair both motor and sensory functions. This is relevant—it identifies the fact that the brain is responsible for controlling the body. Not only were the injuries noted, but also noted the first explanations that were ever recorded of the structures of the brain, as well as how to treat injuries and when to know not to. '

While this particular document did not explain much about behaviorism, it does create a foundation for the idea of psychology and the brain becoming a legitimate medical and, therefore, scientific field. The knowledge involved in this scroll was found to far exceed even Hippocrates, believed to be the founder of modern medicine, who lived 1000 years after the penning of these scrolls.

The First Psychology Experiment

Perhaps the beginning of psychological study, however, came with the experimentation of Lin Xie in the 6th century AD. This experiment sought to understand how vulnerable people were to being distracted, and in particular, they involved the active testing of several people to determine what they were capable of doing when distracted.

In particular, Lin Xie had people drawing a square with one hand while actively drawing a circle with the other in order to determine if they could control both sides of their body in different manners at the same time. While this does not provide much insight to us today, it is commonly believed to be the birth of the study of the mind and what humanity can do as an experimental science. Just as with the Edwin Smith Papyrus, then, this is important to recognize not for the contribution itself, but because it began to set the stage to understand psychology as a science instead of as an aspect of philosophy.

The Vedanta

Moving forward in history, the next major acknowledgment of psychology could be seen in India's *Vedanta*. This was a series of Buddhist philosophical writing that acknowledged the sense of self. In particular, it addressed several concepts that anyone with even a little bit of psychology knowledge would recognize as common psychological keywords. In particular, the Vedanta addressed feelings of the mind in several ways. These were recognizing aggregates, emptiness, the non-self, and mindfulness.

In particular, aggregates encompassed the understanding of five distinct concepts. These were form, sensation, perception, mental formations, and consciousness. Form acknowledged the physical or material existence of anything, in particular in relation to the four elements of earth, water, fire, or wind. Sensation referred to any sort of sensory interaction with objects in ways that are either positive, negative, or neutral. Perception referred to the understanding of a sensory and mental process. Effectively, it allows for the recognition and labeling of something, such as the acknowledgment that the furry little quadrupedal animal in front of you is a cat, or that the plant next to you is the color green. Mental formations refer to the ability to create an understanding of activities. It is the idea of conditioning a feeling or action based upon the exposure to an object. Finally, consciousness refers to an awareness of something around or in front of you, as well as an ability to understand its components.

Abu Zayd Ahmed ibn al-Balkhi and the Psyche

As we move on from India into the Middle-East, we meet a Persian scholar who was particularly interested in science and psychology. He was the first to introduce mental health and mental hygiene, treating them as a method to treat the soul. In particular, he penned *Sustenance for Body and Soul,* calling it a form of spiritual health. In his work, he described that physical and mental health are directly connected to each other, recognizing that spiritual and psychological health are intricately intertwined and that doctors of the day would emphasize too much on the body without ever treating the mind as well.

In particular, he asserted that because of the fact that people are both their soul (or mind) and body, it is important that they must both be healthy. In addition, he was certain that if the body gets sick, then the psyche loses its ability to function, referring to the fact that when you are sick physically, you usually feel exhausted, foggy, and unable to really properly function. If the psyche gets sick, then, of course, the body would also struggle, leading to physical responses to mental illnesses.

Additionally, he was the first to recognize that there is a difference between neurosis and psychosis, asserting that neurosis is distressing, but still allows for functioning, whereas psychosis involves a disconnect between reality and fantasy. He identified four distinct emotional disorders, which you may recognize as being quite similar to several of the more commonly known disorders of today. These were fear and anxiety, anger and aggression, sadness and depression, and obsession. When discussing depression, three types were considered: normal depression, endogenous depression that is a response to something physical, and clinical depression, which is more reactive.

Al-Balkhi also was able to identify treatment for these sicknesses, such as talking through a loss, advising, and counseling, and also internal manners, such as learning to develop other methods of thinking in order to help cope with them. Effectively, this was the first real step toward the psychology that you know today.

The Philosophy of the Mind

Up until relatively recently, psychology was not seen as a science the way that it is today. Rather, it was considered a branch of philosophy until well into the 1800s. If you are familiar with philosophy at all, you may recognize some of the bigger names that are discussed here. Influential philosophers, such as Immanuel Kant, Rene Descartes, David Hume, and John Locke all busied themselves with ways to tackle the mystery of the human mind. Ever the deep thinkers, these philosophers sought to address why we behave the way that we do, coming up with ideas that would become the forefront of modern-day psychology.

Rene Descartes

Even if you are not particularly savvy with philosophers, you are likely familiar with Descartes. Considered the father of modern philosophy, he was responsible for spreading far more than just philosophical ideas or thoughts—he also contributed greatly toward calculus, and more importantly to this book, the idea of dualism: a concept within psychology that recognizes that there is an inherent difference between the mind and the body. Effectively, dualism declares that the mind is one thing that is not physical, compared to the brain, which is physical and recognizes the split between the two.

With his monumental words, "Cogito, ergo sum" (I think; therefore, I am), Descartes tackled the concept of dualism head-on. He recognized that the mind and body had to interact somewhere, believing that the pineal gland was the area through which the mind can interact with the body.

In his work, *The Passions of the Soul*, written in 1646, he declared that there were animal spirits that influenced the human soul—these spirits were known as passions, and there were six that he identified. These were wonder, love, hatred, desire, joy, and sadness. As you can identify, these are quite similar to the universal emotions, missing only a few of them. Effectively, the thought was that the pineal gland served as the connection between the soul (or mind) and body, but the animal spirits could sort of hijack that connection, causing the body to react in ways that are not necessarily intended.

John Locke

Continuing along with the theme of philosophers and psychology, we must now look at John Locke. In particular, he was interested in the cognitive abilities of people. In his *Essay Concerning Human Understanding*, Locke attempted to address the foundation of human knowledge. He determined that the mind was effectively a blank slate at birth, with nothing stored within it. Think of the newborn mind, then, as a brand new hard-drive that has not yet been hooked up to your computer .He then described that, through time, the mind was filled with information and learning via experience. He was determined to reject the commonly accepted idea of innate ideas, such as the idea that all people are born with the ability to do or believe something.

Locke, however, rejected that concept and stated that the idea of innate ideas, such as recognizing something as sweet, comes not because humans innately understand sweetness, but rather because the exposure to sweetness occurs incredibly early on before children are able to begin communicating what they know. Effectively, Locke addressed the idea of learning and knowledge.

David Hume

In the mid-1700s, the continuous pursuit for understanding of the human mind continued with David Hume's *A Treatise of Human Nature*, designed to be a sort of combination between empiricism, skepticism, and naturalism. Effectively,

He discussed the idea of ethics in relation to the mind—he described that people were enslaved to their passions, marking a difference between morality versus reason. Effectively, he wanted to address how and why people make the decisions that they do.

Hume also addressed his own theory of mind and the passions—he determined that what we would refer to as emotions and desires (Hume's "passions") are impressions instead of being ideas. The passions felt, fear, grief, joy, hope, aversion, and desire, come directly in response from pain or pleasure. Further, his indirect passions, such as pride, shame, love, and hate, are a bit more complex and indirect—unlike the passions listed previously, indirect passions do not drive behavior but rather influence thinking.

This can be summarized as attempting to identify how our feelings toward situations determine behaviors. While there is far more to Hume than just learning about emotions, this is the most relevant portion to the furthering of psychology.

Immanuel Kant

German philosopher Immanuel Kant helped propel psychology even closer to becoming its own proper discipline through his own writing. Kant felt that psychology of his own day was far too out of touch with true human experience, focusing too much on internal processes. Instead, he sought to look into how the mind worked. He wanted to answer questions about how knowledge is attained, how much we can know about an object, or how we could even learn to begin with.

In the psychology of his time, knowledge was nothing but a replication of the external world within the mind. However, Kant acknowledged that the mind is far too complex to simply be a reflection for sensory input, and instead said that we gain knowledge through cognitive faculties. Effectively, we learn from our environment, but what we learn is not exactly what we see in front of us—it must be interpreted. The mind does not just learn—it receives input, understands that input, processes that input, and then learns from it, all of which are united by the sense of self. Effectively, the mind is a conglomerate of all of the mental faculties coming together.

From Philosophical to Scientific

Eventually, the bridge from philosophy to its own discipline arose. Up until the mid-1800s, it was seen as little more than theory, left to the philosophers to debate and understand amidst their politics and metaphysics. However, over time, it became clear that psychology varied greatly from true philosophy. While both were endlessly fascinated with understanding why something happened or how it worked, psychology was not dependent upon logic. Philosophy itself is an incredibly logic-driven field—everything must fit within certain boundaries, and if they do not fit within those boundaries, then they are likely to be rejected from philosophical discussion.

However, as psychology grew more and more complex, with questions to consider, such as why some people tended to behave one way in response to one thing, but another person would respond entirely different, it became clear that psychology would require more than just logic and observation. It required experimentation.

It was the growing understanding of physiology as well as the need for scientific studies that began to really propel psychology into its own discipline, entirely separate from philosophy. It became clear that the continued study of the mind would require that level of scientific structure toward it, as seen through the work of the mid-1800s German physiologist, Wilhelm Wundt.

Wilhelm Wundt and the Principles of Physiological Psychology

In 1874, Wundt published a book known as *Principles of Physiological Psychology*. This was largely considered to be one of the first links between physiology and the study of human cognition and behavior. His opening of the world's first psychology lab in 1879 became known as the beginning of psychology of its own, and he began to push for empirical studies.

Wundt focused on psychology as the study of consciousness, using experiments in order to study mental processes. The only way that this was possible at the time was through the use of introspection. Introspection was the act of informal reflection, as well as what Wundt defined as the process of experimental self-observation. Effectively, he would take several people and then train them to become their own psychologists; he taught them how to carefully analyze their own thoughts as free from judgment or bias as possible.

Of course, most people see Wundt's methods of gathering data to be about as far from unbiased as they could be—after all, there is no way to truly monitor the inner workings of someone else's mind in order to test for veracity, and because of that, his methods today would likely be rejected as unscientific, but there is no doubt that this research was monumental in propelling psychology into its own discipline.

Wundt's lab educated an estimated 17,000 students, spreading the idea of psychology as its own concept far and wide. It is undeniable that, while many of his ideas were disconfirmed and made less influential over time, his own actions did act as the catalyst in the shift toward scientific psychology.

The Spread of Psychology

With Wundt's spread of psychology through his educational lab, several other branches began to pop up as well. In particular, two became notable in the progress of psychology: Structuralism and functionalism. These were the first two schools in a chain of many that psychology would grow to see. They provided paradigms through which to look at the impact of psychology, using several common rules and thoughts that would guide the process.

Edward Titchener and Structuralism

Structuralism became the first school of thought of psychology. Within this school of thought, it was believed that the consciousness could be divided into smaller components, and through understanding those components, you would be able to begin to understand the mind. Like Wundt, Titchener made use of introspection as the primary mode of collecting data.

Titchener made it a point to use several aspects of Wundt's psychology, though it all had his own spin.

Unfortunately, structuralism never really took hold in the field, and as Titchener eventually died, so too did structuralism.

William James and Functionalism

With the rise of one school of psychology, several others began to pop up as well, all vying for the domination of the field. In almost a direct response and challenge to Titchener's structuralism came functionalism. One of the first major American psychologists, William James, wrote a book known as *The Principles of Psychology*. With this book, he managed to dominate the American psychology field, and his book very quickly became the new standard that was used. The information within this book was not directly titled to be functionalism, but it did serve as the basis for the school of thought.

As functionalism came onto the scene, it brought about an understanding of how behaviors function. IN particular, it cared about learning how behaviors benefit anyone at all. They sought to see how certain behaviors were conducive to the situation while others were far less so. Effectively, while both structuralism and functionalism emphasized the study of the unconscious mind, functionalism prioritized looking at consciousness as a continuous process through which everything was processed.

Functionalism, too, died off after a while, though the theories left behind were still quite influential.

The Rise of Psychoanalysis

In the late 1800s, another familiar name to most people entered the limelight: Sigmund Freud. An Austrian neurologist, he became the founder of psychoanalysis. What set psychoanalysis apart from its counterparts was primarily the ability to begin therapeutically treating issues that have arisen. Effectively, the idea of psychoanalysis pushes forth the idea of the unconscious mind that drives everything, and in taking information from the unconscious to the conscious part of the mind, you can achieve catharsis—the ability to cope with the issue at hand.

Effectively, Freud founded what would become one of the most influential aspects of modern psychology: The art of therapy. The principles of psychoanalysis very closely align with what you would see in modern techniques such as cognitive behavioral therapy, in which it is believed that unconscious thoughts influence your feelings, which drive certain behaviors, and that you can begin to restructure those thoughts into something more functional if you were to bring them to the conscious mind to address them.

Psychoanalysis brought with it the psychodynamic approach to psychology, stepping away from the ideas of the past and instead focusing on the fact that the mind has several aspects to it that must be considered.

Today, many of Freud's own aspects are considered quite outdated, such as believing that everything is motivated by sex and sexual aggression. However, the principles he used in treating other people remain incredibly influential in today's psychology.

And with that, we have arrived at the first of the modern perspectives of psychology. That was an overview of thousands of years of development, taking psychology from theoretical philosophy to a hard science that is driven by evidence, numbers, and the scientific method.

Chapter 2: What is Psychology?

With the history of psychology behind us, it is time to begin to delve into the understanding of psychology as a field. Psychology itself is incredibly influential—it is necessary to be able to understand the mind in order to truly treat the mind. As we learn more and more about the mind, it becomes imperative that our ability to study it grows as well. Whereas before, it was assumed that some sort of emotional upset was a direct result of a demon or spirit, it is now known to be caused by other causes, such as personality disorders or mental illnesses. Sometimes, it is biological in nature, such as having a physical structure of the brain that is different, while other times, it involves learned responses to a situation or to stimuli.

Nevertheless, psychology itself, as a study of the mind, is critical to learn. As it is learned and developed, we gain so much more insight into what is going on with other people. We learn to acknowledge what holds other people back and what drives them forward. We see what drives people to behave altruistically or to take care of their family, and what drives them to harm others. To understand psychology is to understand being human and to understand being human is to be able to understand how to treat others with kindness and empathy.

The Study of the Mind

By definition, psychology is the scientific study of the mind and behavior, and it has done that. However, there is so much to the mind and behavior; think of all of the fields within psychology that exist. There are fields dedicated to understanding normal human development, seeing how children grow and learn. Other fields look at abnormal psychology and take a look at how it matters and how to treat it. Some people study how to learn, while others look at how drugs and other substances may impact the body and mind. At the end of the day, psychology covers anything to do with the mind, both mentally and physically.

Psychology achieves this by having four main goals: To describe, explain, predict, and change the way that people think and act. We will go over each of these goals in a moment, but what is critical to understand here is that these goals drive psychology forward. They make it clear that we act in certain manners for certain reasons and see, to figure it out in order to make any changes if necessary.

Describe

The first goal is to describe behaviors and thought processes. This is critical if you want to be able to understand general rules that are typically exhibited in behavior. For example, if you want to be able to tell how someone is going to behave, you would look at several instances that show exactly how they are going to behave. We observe infants playing to figure out that at some point, something changes and they no longer think that something ceases to exist when it is out of sight. We watch how children interact with each other without guidance to identify when altruistic behavior starts to develop.

Describing and observing create a critical first step precisely because they are responsible for developing a base understanding of standard behavior. In being able to analyze, you must figure out a base norm in order to figure out where the deviations from the norm are.

Explain

After being able to describe the processes of other people, explaining is the second goal. Upon being able to describe what occurs, such as watching the infants seem to come to the realization that, even when mom and dad are out of sight, they still exist, the law can start to be assembled. They can start to figure out *why* this happens. This is what happens during the second goal of psychology—explaining.

Usually, this goal involves understanding what happened—it looks at the description of what has happened in the describe stage and then begins to come up with several theories that may or may not support it. These theories are meant to come up with whatever the explanation is for that particular behavior.

Effectively, the psychologists will try to figure out the most reasonable explanation for why someone does something and then tries to test it.

Predict

As the empirical research yields potential explanations for the behavior being studied, psychology then moves toward prediction as the primary goal. During this stage, the explanations created in the previous step are taken and tested. If they fail to meet expectations, they are removed from the list, and they will try to come up with something else.

For example, assume that you have been watching your child seem utterly baffled when you disappear and reappear playing peekaboo. You can then assume that your child thinks that you are gone when you disappear. You then predict that your child will react with the same sense of bafflement when you take that ball that he was playing with and cover it up with a blanket because the child will be looking for his ball. You test this out, and sure enough, your explanation was correct.

Change

Finally, once you have been able to describe, explain, and predict the behaviors, you can then begin to understand how to influence change in other people. You may look to help control a negative behavior, such as someone who suffers from anxiety learning to cope with those feelings. You may make it a point to look at someone who has obsessive-compulsive disorder, figure out their triggers, and then figure out how best to help them change that behavior.

Effectively, change allows for behaviors to be modified in order for people to develop healthy coping mechanisms, even when they are faced with difficult situations, disorders, or struggles that make otherwise normal functioning difficult. You can learn how to overcome phobias once you can understand and predict the cause, or you can learn to fix issues with emotional regulation. You can challenge depression. You can correct negative thoughts. You can effectively begin treating the other person's mind when you know how the mind is implicated.

The study of psychology can largely be broken down into five distinct perspectives—each wishes to focus on an entirely different part of the mind. These different perspectives are the biological perspective, the psychodynamic perspective, the behavioral perspective, the cognitive perspective, and the humanistic perspective. Effectively, someone who looks at an issue such as depression from the biological perspective is going to be focused on the biology behind the depression being studied—it will look at neurotransmitters and areas of the brain that are responsible for the feelings. However, someone in the behavioral perspective may be looking for the way that the external world is directly responsible for influencing those feelings of depression.

We will take a look at all five of these perspectives to get a solid working idea of all aspects of what is happening within the mind. While having one specific focus can be incredibly useful, it takes all five to put together a proper, complete view of what is happening.

The Biological Perspective

As you may have assumed, the biological approach is all about how your body impacts your mind. In particular, it is an attempt to understand the link between the mental states and body of someone else. If you are feeling happy, what is going on in the body? There is a physiological change in response to your feelings, and the biological perspective is incredibly interested in looking into it. Effectively, then, you will be looking into how the brain works.

Within the biological perspective, effectively, you and your consciousness are all the collective sum of your body. Your brain all comes together to work through electrical impulses and chemicals, and those tiny impulses are what create you. In the great debate of nature vs. nurture, this is the nature part. It believes that the biology of the brain and body are what are important in determining the behaviors and thoughts of the other person.

Just like the other perspectives, the biological perspective is entirely interested in understanding people and their behaviors. However, they want to look at other aspects. Genetics come into play, as do physical changes to the brain. They may take a special interest in how genetics influence all sorts of aspects of personality, like depression or anxiety, or how brain damage can lead to several issues in ability or behavior. In particular, biological psychologists will look into identical twins, learning as much as they can about the tendencies of people versus what they actually do.

When you are using the biological perspective, you are likely going to use tools to observe the brain as directly as possible.

Scans such as a PET or MRI can allow psychologists to view the brain's physical structure in order to begin to make inferences on the behavioral aspects of the person.

In particular, the biological perspective is a powerful one to take—when you use the biological perspective, you are effectively ensuring that you understand the physiology, and sometimes, that is enough. If you know that someone has suffered from a massive stroke and can see exactly where the damage is, for example, you can begin to predict exactly what parts of their behavior are likely to be impacted. It also means that certain behavioral changes may be approached as a sign of a physical medical issue, such as a brain injury or a tumor.

This is also the perspective that would be responsible for ensuring that medication is effective. When the physiological cause is understood, it becomes far easier to begin identifying how best to medicate the issue. If there are certain parts of the brain that are struggling to create enough of a certain neurotransmitter, for example, then that can be medicated for in order to help the body to then help the mind.

The Psychodynamic Perspective

The psychodynamic approach began with Sigmund Freud's psychoanalysis, but it did grow over time to encompass several other theories as well, such as the theories of Karl Jung, Erik Erikson, and Alfred Adler. Within the psychodynamic theory, it is believed that early childhood events influence almost everything. Effectively, during the early childhood period, you are particularly susceptible to being damaged and therefore internalizing issues within your unconscious mind. These lead to behavioral problems that are the results of the unconscious mind.

In particular, you will see within the psychodynamic perspective; the emphasis is placed on the unconscious mind. Think of the mind like an iceberg—only the tip is visible. You can see the conscious part of the mind or the tip of the iceberg, but the vast majority of it is hidden beneath the surface of the water. Effectively, the unconscious mind houses almost everything. All of your motivational impulses are housed in the unconscious. Your feelings will come from it, your motives will be rooted in it, and your decisions will be based upon it.

The unconscious mind, while incredibly powerful, is also incredibly impressionable. This, then, pushes the focus of human behavior from nature to nurture.

Further, within the psychodynamic perspective, you see three parts of personality that arise: The id, the ego, and the super-ego.

Your id refers to the instincts—it is inherited and holds all of your natural personality and behavioral tendencies. Your ego is the part of the mind that is meant to sort of mitigate the demands and desires of the id, which is primarily quite unrealistic, and the world around you. This is the part that makes decisions. Finally, the superego is the series of values and morals that are learned from both society and parents.

The id and super-ego are considered the unconscious mind—they both fight to win the favor of the mind (ego). Effectively, your instinctive tendencies toward sex and aggressive behavior will constantly be trying to get you to act impulsively, while the learned portion is trying to keep you in line in order to guarantee that you will not do something that you should not be.

The conflict leads to anxiety, which the ego must cope with somehow. These coping mechanisms become the method through which you behave. Effectively, then, the conscious mind is the slave for the unconscious mind, with the unconscious mind making the decisions and controlling. However, the unconscious mind is also influenced regularly by external features and instances. A trauma can, for example, lead to a change in the unconscious mind, which is then noticeable in the behavior.

The Behavioral Perspective

The behavioral perspective places emphasis on the environment on your behaviors. It asserts that you can effectively be trained to do just about anything if someone is willing to put in the effort to do so. When you believe in the behavioral perspective, you reject the idea of free will—you effectively declare that all behavior is learned through either reinforcements or punishment.

Reinforcements refer to consequences that occur after a behavior that is either positive or negative. Positive refers to the fact that something was put in place, whereas negative refers to the act of something being removed. In this case, positive reinforcement is a pleasant situation that is added to encourage the behavior to continue. A negative reinforcement, then, is a situation being removed, usually an unpleasant one, in response to a behavior in order to encourage it to continue happening in the future.

On the other hand, punishment is the act of something happening to discourage a behavior. It is the opposite of reinforcement in the sense that it is designed to be discouraging while reinforcement is enforcing. Like reinforcement, punishment can be both positive and negative. For example, positive punishment could entail adding extra chores in retaliation for not listening or lying about a situation. On the other hand, negative reinforcement is the act of removing something pleasing in order to deter the behavior in the future. For example, imagine that your teen daughter has not turned in several assignments, and she has her cell phone taken away until she gets them all in. You took away something pleasant, in this case, her cell phone, in order to discourage the behavior of continuing to miss assignments.

Behaviorists believe that the above processes are what cause behavior to continue or discontinue. When you enjoy a situation or get something pleasant in response, you want to encourage doing something. When you realize that you have the same bad response every time you try to do something, you are going to learn not to do that behavior any more out of wanting to avoid the negative stimulus. Effectively, in behaviorism, thoughts do not matter—behaviors do. It does not matter how angry someone is about the consequences or how unfair your child believes losing her cell phone was—all that matters is the end result.

The Cognitive Perspective

Cognitive psychologists, on the other hand, assert that behavior is determined due to expectations. You have a certain thought about a situation and expect it to behave that way. Effectively, then, you make expectations that are informed based upon what you already know and try to make the proper inferences in your behavior. In this instance, you are solving problems and interacting with the world based on the memory of what has happened in the past. You assume that what has happened in the past will happen again in the future, or you make assumptions based on similar events.

This takes humanity away from the idea of being completely devoid of free will and instead as something that is capable of thoughts and feelings again. Of course, this also brings with it far more complication than was present otherwise.

Imagine that you have plans to go out with friends for the night. You assume that the night will be full of fun—you and your friends would leave the kids at home, go to a movie, and then have dinner and a few drinks at your favorite restaurant. You get yourself all dressed up and ready, but when you arrive at the meeting place, you realize that two of your three friends have brought their children with them, which means that movie that you have wanted to see is no longer on the table, nor is having a few drinks with dinner, as there are little eyes there.

In this instance, you are probably quite disappointed. You had certain expectations, only to have them completely overthrown, and that can be incredibly difficult for some people to cope with. However, according to cognitivists, you are not disappointed because of the fact that your friends brought their children along to what was supposed to be a kid-free event—you are annoyed because your own expectations were completely and utterly thrown out the window. The fact that the instance did not line up with your own expectations is why you are annoyed and disappointed. It is that thought process and the disconnect that is the root of the disappointment, not the fact that the other parties did something unexpected.

This is where the idea of other people not being responsible for your own feelings comes from—only your own thoughts can influence your behavior, and no one else is responsible for them. Even if someone else does not live up to your own expectations, it is your own job to figure out how to manage that disappointment.

The Humanistic Perspective

Finally, the humanistic approach to psychology emphasizes that humans are motivated by their own inherent goodness. Effectively, people need to be empowered in order to become the best person that they are able to be. They want to offer support without the guidance, to empower individuals to make their own decisions.

Humanistic psychology approaches the situation in a way that directly rejects those behaviorist and psychodynamic approaches that are believed to be too limiting. Instead, people are believed to be entirely free to make their own decisions, and inherently, they will always strive to be better. Those who use the humanistic approach emphasize the idea that people will actively work toward improvement, seeking to overcome difficult situations in order to attain what is known as self-actualization—satisfaction in life.

Effectively, the driving force behind behaviors is not the brain or the environment, but rather the inherent drive people have to better themselves and their situation. Of course, this comes with its own implications as well—humanistic studies inherently reject scientific methodology. They instead focus on qualitative research, like discussing situations. These are effectively useful for individual studies to understand an individual person without trying to figure out the entirety of humankind's behavior.

Chapter 3: Emotional Intelligence and Psychology

With the basics out of the way, it is time to begin discussing emotional intelligence. Emotional intelligence is incredibly trendy these days, and for great reason. Emotional intelligence itself has been used in several capacities, even before it was ever defined. It determines whether you are able to interact well with others or whether people will like you. It determines your successes, as well as how you move forward in improving in the future.

Ultimately, nearly every behavior that you have is believed to be rooted in some way to your emotional intelligence, particularly from a cognitive perspective. Essentially, if your emotional intelligence acts as a driving motivator, you can begin to predict how people will behave based on how emotionally intelligent they are.

What holds true no matter how much or little emotional intelligence someone has, it is primarily a skillset, and as a skillset, it can be developed and learned over time. You can learn to become emotionally intelligent, even if you are not naturally. You can spend the time to develop these skills in order to become the emotionally intelligent individual that you wish to be.

Within this chapter, we will discuss what emotional intelligence is, touching upon the main purposes of emotional intelligence, the pillars of emotional intelligence, and how emotional intelligence relates to psychology concepts, such as emotions, empathy, and communication. As you read through these chapters, try to think about yourself. Do you have these skills that are being discussed? Do you feel like you are lacking in the empathy department, or perhaps that your communication could be better? If you think that you may struggle with your emotional intelligence, this is perhaps one of the most straightforward parts of yourself to work on.

Defining Emotional Intelligence

Before we begin, let's create a working definition of emotional intelligence. Primarily, emotional intelligence is the ability to do three things. It involves being able to understand emotions, regulate your own emotions, and use your ability to understand emotions to manage and facilitate your relationships with other people. When you are emotionally intelligent, effectively, you are able to actively harness these abilities in order to achieve a high leadership potential. When you have that high leadership potential, you find that you are more capable and confident when you interact with other people.

Effectively, emotional intelligence is largely able to determine whether you are able to understand your own emotions while still being able to regulate and influence the emotions of others as well. This skill is one that is critical to interpersonal relationships for several reasons—it determines how you approach other people. It determines how you are able to communicate with other people. It determines how likely you are to being annoyed by other people's actions or inactions.

Emotional intelligence is effectively the pinnacle of emotional maturity—when you learn to be emotionally intelligent, you are resilient and in control. You will be able to manage those difficult emotions, such as anger or sadness. You will be able to sense these signals in other people as well and act accordingly in order to help mitigate the negative effects or behaviors. You will be able to solve conflicts with other people with ease, and you will be just in tune enough with other people's emotions to ensure that you are always helping people in the way that they need.

People who are highly emotionally intelligent are incredibly skilled when it comes to being able to interact with other people, and this makes them incredibly desirable in relationships, workplaces, and as leaders. When you are emotionally intelligent, people will naturally flock to you, as they feel that you are trustworthy, confident, and charismatic enough to be a proper leader.

The Pillars of Emotional Intelligence

Ultimately, one of the simplest methods of understanding emotional intelligence and the skills it entails is through looking at emotional intelligence as a series of pillars. These are sorts of clusters of behavior that you will look at in order to get a better idea of the skills they entail. Emotional intelligence is commonly considered to have four pillars of emotional intelligence: Self-awareness, self-regulation, social awareness, and emotional regulation. Each of these four pillars is critical to understanding if you ever hope to master emotional intelligence for yourself.

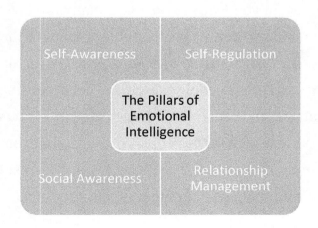

Self-Awareness

The first of the pillars is self-awareness. As you may imagine, it entails your ability to check into your own emotional state at any given moment. Many people struggle to ever truly understand their emotions—they feel good or bad, but beyond that, they are unsure what they are feeling. This is unfortunate, as feelings have far more nuances than just good or bad. When you know exactly what you are feeling, you will be able to understand yourself better, recognizing your motivations and why you are doing what you are doing.

Beyond just being aware of the emotional states, self-awareness also encompasses the ability to be aware of your own abilities in an accurate fashion. When you are able to identify your own abilities accurately, you know what you are capable of, as well as what you struggle with, and knowing this enables you to build up a reasonable, accurate, logical understanding of who you are as a person. You will know what you need to work on and what you are capable of, so you never volunteer to do more than you can handle.

Self-awareness also entails the ability to be self-confident. You will effectively be able to trust yourself because you are so in-tune with your abilities. Effectively, knowing how you behave enables you to recognize when you should trust yourself to do something. If you can trust yourself to do something, you come across as more trustworthy to others. After all, it is incredibly difficult to trust someone that you do not know to do something for you or for other people.

Self-Awareness

- Emotional Self-awareness
- Accurate self-assessment
- Self-confidence

Self-Regulation

Self-regulation is the second of the pillars of emotional intelligence. When you are able to use self-regulation, you are able to manage your own emotions. With self-control, you are able to make sure that your emotions are always expressed in a method that is effective and appropriate. If you express your emotions in a way that is less than appropriate, or if you give in to whatever emotional impulses you feel, you are likely to burn bridges in relationships rather quickly, making this a critical skill. As satisfying as it may feel in the moment to scream at a customer, it would not be so satisfying to lose your job as a result.

On top of that ability to control yourself, the ability to self-regulate involves plenty about your own intrinsic motivations. Those who are skilled at self-regulation tend to be achievement-oriented and self-motivated. This means that they are able to work toward their goals with their own initiative. When you are willing to be self-motivated, you show that you are willing to work through setbacks, even if those setbacks are such problems as procrastination and simply not being motivated to work.

Self-regulation also comes with the ability to be transparent—you are open and honest when you are able to self-regulate. You may know that what you are saying or doing is less popular, but you trust yourself and that you are making the right decision by telling other people the truth. This brings with it a sense of trustworthiness. When you are trustworthy, other people are going to naturally feel like you are more approachable.

Self-regulation, because it also involves the ability to control your own emotions, also brings with it the ability to become adaptable—you know that change happens sometimes, and you are willing and able to cope with it. You are able to manage your own expectations, even when they do not come into fruition. You know that there is plenty to learn from plans changing, even if they changed due to failure, and you are optimistic enough to keep hoping for the best.

Social Awareness

The third pillar of emotional intelligence is social awareness. This is the ability to understand other people. This skillset is critical if you want to be able to interact meaningfully with other people. If you want to be able to communicate with others, you need to be able to understand them, and that is the entire purpose of social awareness. Social awareness comes with three major skills: the ability to empathize, the ability of organizational awareness, and developing a service orientation.

Empathy itself is the ability to connect with other people in a way that allows for the acknowledgment and understanding of their feelings. It is critical in relating to other people. You need to be able to acknowledge other people's emotions if you wish to be able to understand people's emotions, and you are not likely to be able to acknowledge the emotions of other people if you do not first understand your own feelings.

Organizational awareness refers to your ability to manage how you explain yourself to others. It is effectively your ability to make sure that you are always speaking at a level that is readily understood by other people. You are able to ensure that the comprehension levels of those around you always line up with being just right. Think about how a presentation geared toward kindergarteners would go if it were given to high schoolers—they would not bother paying attention to it because it would be far too simple to be worth listening to. Likewise, if you were to deliver that same presentation to a bunch of kindergarteners despite being meant for high schoolers, the children probably will not understand very much. When you are able to use organizational awareness, however, you will be able to ensure that you are always speaking to the proper audience whenever you are trying to speak to someone else, allowing you to retain attention longer and more effectively.

Finally, a service orientation refers to just how willing you are to help other people. It involves being willing to contribute to the efforts while also showing that you are happily willing to help guide your group to your desired goal. When you use this, you are able to make sure that you listen effectively as well.

- Empathy
- Organizational Awareness
- Service Orientation

Relationship Management

The final pillar of emotional intelligence is relationship management. This particular pillar refers to the ability to manage relationships and influence other people. In order to develop relationship management, however, you must first develop all of the other pillars. Relationship management requires you to be intricately aware of your own emotions and behaviors, as well as able to control them. It requires you to have a solid understanding of other people as well. The skills in relationship management include being able to inspire leadership, influence others, manage conflict, trigger change, develop others, and be skilled in teamwork.

Relationship management creates inspirational leaders who are capable of leading other people. Whether a leader through authority or respect or working as a mentor to other people, this skill is critical if you want to be able to manage others. This is what makes people willing to follow you in the first place.

Influence allows those skilled at relationship management to ensure that they can convince other people to do what needs to be done. They are persuasive, articulate, motivating, and able to call people to action with ease. This skill is critical in leading others, as if you cannot get other people to do what they need to, you cannot lead them.

Conflict management grants these individuals the ability to manage the relationships with other people, either interpersonally, or between two other people. They are able to facilitate the necessary communication between people to ensure that everyone is able to leave a situation feeling like they have been listened to and supported .Effectively, conflict management allows for the ending of arguments or opinions by ensuring that everyone ends up on the same page.

The relationship manager is able to facilitate change in the world, even if it means that they have to be the catalyst for that change. They are willing to support any change that is necessary, even if that means they must take a difficult or uncomfortable position. They will do anything that is necessary to make that change happen.

Because of the unique position of the leader, you need to be able to understand how other people interact with each other. If you can see two people that are interacting with each other in a certain way, you can usually begin to figure out who works best with whom. Being able to understand how people interact means that you can put together teams effectively, and being able to see the skills of other people means you will be able to point them in the right direction to ensure that everyone is always growing and moving toward their greatest potentials.

Finally, the leader must be willing and able to work with other people effectively, no matter what happens. This requires an ability to cope readily and easily with any change that may arise.

- Inspirational leadership
- Influetial
- Conflict manager
- Change catalyst
- Developing others
- Teamwork and collaboration

Emotions and Emotional Intelligence

Emotions and emotional intelligence are intricately combined just by virtue of both being involved in the act of feeling and acknowledging emotions. As you have seen, emotions are sort of the primary backbone to the entire process of emotional intelligence. You must begin with understanding your own emotions if you want to be able to progress past that first stage of self-awareness, and without that awareness of your own emotions, you cannot ever hope to understand other people. If you cannot understand other people, how can you hope to ensure that other people are actively and readily willing and able to listen to you as a leader? If you cannot touch base with your own emotions, how can you expect other people to be willing to put up with you and your dramatics if any conflict were to ever arise?

What is important to note is that despite the fact that emotional intelligence is primarily focused on behaving in ways that are not emotionally impulsive, it is not seeking out a blanket ban on emotions in general. In fact, emotional intelligence strongly encourages people to feel their emotions whenever possible and relevant. When you feel your emotions, you feel what your body and unconscious mind want you to. Your emotions, as you will learn in Chapter 4, are incredibly important. They serve a valuable purpose in keeping you regulated, and because of that, they should never be completely ignored or disregarded.

Rather than disregarding emotions, emotional intelligence seeks to regulate the act of behaving impulsively in response. When you are able to become emotionally intelligent, you will effectively be learning how to stop when you do feel strong emotions so you can regulate them out. You will be able to prevent yourself from acting in an inappropriate manner.

Imagine for a moment that you are incredibly angry—perhaps you just found out that your child broke your watch that was gifted to you by your late father. You are absolutely furious, as that was the last precious belonging of his that you had, and now it's broken. If you are emotionally intelligent, you acknowledge that anger—you allow yourself to feel those emotions because being able to feel emotions is important to finding some sort of closure or resolution. However, despite acknowledging your anger and continuing to feel it, you are able to remind yourself that reacting in anger is hardly the right decision here. You remind yourself that acting in anger would do nothing but upset your child, how did not intentionally break the watch. It had been an unfortunate accident, and your child was devastated about it. You could see that much looking at his face.

When you are able to acknowledge your emotions, recognizing the value that they bring to the table, you can use them to inform yourself. You can use the feeling of that emotion as your unconscious cue to remind yourself to slow down, relax, and continue moving forward. Effectively, you can make sure that you are able to use your emotions and the knowledge that you are feeling that emotion in order to help yourself self-regulate.

Beyond just that, however, imagine that you are aware of other people's emotions. Keeping in mind that emotions are indicative of a need that is currently going unmet when you are able to use emotional intelligence in order to better enable yourself to read the feelings of those around you, you are also able to understand the needs of those around you who may need your help sooner rather than later. When you can understand the needs of other people, you are also able to understand far more. You can understand how best to ensure that other people have their needs met, and with that, you can become an effective leader.

Emotions are critical—we feel them for incredibly important reasons and attempting to disregard them, even when we are trying to think with a rational mindset, is doing a disservice to those around you.

Emotional Intelligence and Empathy

Empathy is one of the most critical skills in emotional intelligence. While being able to identify your own emotions is always important, what matters more in many cases is whether you can empathize. This is what bridges the gap from focusing on yourself to being able to accurately interact with others.

If you look at the four pillars of emotional intelligence once more, you may notice that two of the pillars are focused on the self while the other two are directed outwards toward others. The way that you move from the self to the others is through being able to empathize.

For example, imagine that you are able to recognize your own emotional states. You are quite confident in your ability to understand how you are feeling—you have learned the body language you need to know. You have figured out how best to identify when to step in and intervene on your own emotional outbursts. You know what your most common emotional triggers are. But, can you understand what other people are feeling?

Being able to understand your own feeling is not a sudden ability to understand others as well—being able to understand the emotions of others requires empathy, but in order to really understand the feedback that you get via empathy, you must also understand your own emotional state as well.

Forms of Empathy

Empathy itself is defined as the ability to relate to other people, and it exists primarily in three different forms. You can empathize cognitively, emotionally, or compassionately. When you empathize cognitively, you understand the other person's feelings from a straightforward perspective—you know what they are feeling simply because you recognize the signs. However, there is no emotional attachment on your part. You do not particularly care what the other person has that particular feeling—you simply know that they do.

When you empathize emotionally, however, you are able to understand the feelings of the other person as well through feeling it yourself. You are effectively relating to the other person so much that you are able to feel the same way. You see someone suffering, and you feel their pain as if it were your own. Even if you are not doing this unintentionally, most of the time, emotional empathy involves you automatically put yourself in the position of the other person in your mind. You know that you would be sad and scared if you had nowhere to live, and winter was rapidly approaching.

When you empathize compassionately, which is the form of empathy that emotional intelligence emphasizes, you are effectively combining the previous two. You understand the person's feelings cognitively, allowing you to have a solid idea of the feelings of the other person. You are also able to understand the other person's emotions as you relate to them. When you empathize both cognitively and emotionally, you are often driven to emotional empathy—this drives you to act in some way. Feeling both cognitive and emotional relationship to the other person encourages you to act in some way to ensure that they are taken care of as well. You want to help them; however, you can to ensure that you can actively meet their needs to alleviate their suffering. There is rarely any motive for you other than to help. Your compassionate empathy is a sort of call to action that you obey in order to ensure that you actively meet the needs of those around you.

The Purpose of Empathy

Empathy primarily has two purposes that are both directly related to emotional intelligence: It acts as a way through which you can self-regulate, and it acts as a means of communication, primarily of nonverbal emotional signs. When you are able to empathize, then you are able to regulate, as well as read the signs in order to better understand the needs of those around you.

However, before delving into that, consider for a moment *why* we would need to feel empathy in any degree. What does empathy do for you? Why does it matter? The answer is quite simple—we are a social species. In fact, nearly all of emotional intelligence is only relevant because we are a social species. When you live in a group setting, whether that is a family unit, a neighborhood, a tribe, or an entire city or town, you must be able to communicate. Humans, because we depend on others for survival, need to be able to communicate with others clearly.

Think about humans "in the wild" for a moment—we are discussing human beings that have not yet made a move toward modern civilizations. We are specifically discussing the humans that had no choice but to hunt and grow their own food to survive. They had to exist in groups. Humans would hunt in groups with other people as well, allowing them to take down larger prey, which is critical when you consider how much weaker humans are compared to other animals. Humans had to rely on their tribes to help provide protection and to hunt. They relied on each other to live and traveled in these sort of tribes.

Empathy allowed for nonverbal communication to be used. When you are running with a group of people in many life-or-death situations, you are going to want to understand the emotions of those around you, as those emotions will provide you with all sorts of information. You will be able to tell that those around you are scared when there is danger, or sad when they need help. However, even further than that, you can see what their needs are to help them meet them. You will be driven to act because you can feel the needs of the other person, and you are willing to help.

When you are willing to help, you encourage the other person to be willing to help you whenever you find yourself caught in a moment of need. Altruism, that behavior of helping someone else at no benefit, and quite possibly a detriment to yourself is only an effective trait in a species that is primarily altruistic, so empathy keeps us on the right track. You know that you need to make sure that those around you are cared for and fed, so you make sure that you always have enough food to share. Of course, if you were to ever fall on tough times, then they would be more than happy to reciprocate and share with you.

Beyond just survival, however, empathy can benefit interpersonal relationships as well. When you are able to empathize with other people, you know how to manage yourself around the other person. Think back to the example about your child breaking your father's watch—you could see that your child was upset and feeling guilty about the situation, and being able to see the look in your child's eyes helped to remind you to ensure that you did not snap at them or judge them in a way that would be harmful to them. You self-regulated in direct response to empathizing with your child.

Another example of this could be in action having a discussion with someone. Perhaps you are trying to figure out how best to make something work. Your partner keeps suggesting things, but you shoot down each and every one of her ideas. You continue to shut them down simply because they do not make sense given the context, and in doing so, you effectively end up stressing her out. You can see that she is starting to get stressed out, and you can feel those familiar pangs of empathy, and you are able to realize what is going on: You are causing the stress. You are being too controlling and need to somehow otherwise regulate what you are doing.

You then are able to scale it back and make several concessions for your partner, allowing your partner to stop stressing out nearly as much. When you do this, you make sure that your partner is taken care of. You ensure that your partner feels valued instead of stressed out. In being able to recognize that your own emotions were causing some serious stress or other negative emotion in someone else, you can begin to pull it back and ensure that you do not continue to behave in harmful ways.

Emotional Intelligence and Communication

Emotional intelligence also has a significant impact on communication abilities. This makes sense—you cannot possibly be influential if you have no manner through which to communicate somehow with other people. With the increased awareness of how your own emotional feelings can alter your speaking and body language patterns, you can then begin to monitor this. If you know that you are stressed out, you may be able to use your emotional intelligence skills to ensure that you are actively behaving in ways that will serve you well. You will be able to take that extra pause to communicate clearly because you are aware of your tendencies.

Communication then gets more effective simply because you are able to better regulate yourself. You know that you are speaking too rapidly because you are stressed out, so you manually take control and deliberately speak in a slower, more controlled manner. Doing this takes away the power of your anxiety in the first place, allowing you to communicate clearly.

Ultimately, just as developing emotional intelligence was critical in the building of empathy, it is critical in communication settings as well. You must be able to be emotionally intelligent if you want to communicate in the most effective manner possible. Remember, the best way to keep yourself levelheaded when stressed out is by making a point to take a deep breath in and out before speaking to answer the question.

As one final note, remember that you can use your emotions to your benefit. You can leverage your emotions to allow you to communicate clearly. Remember, your emotions are not a sign of weakness, nor do they require total elimination. There are times and places to utilize your emotions, and if you find that the current situation is an appropriate one, you should absolutely make use of those emotions yourself. Doing so allows you to make your point even clearer, and if your emotions are appropriate ones to whatever the situation that you are communicating about, your own display of emotions can help you further emphasize your point and how passionate you are.

Chapter 4: Emotions and Psychological State

Emotional states are critical to understand when you are talking about person-to-person contact. Emotions can strongly complicate nearly everything about your interaction with someone else, changing how they are approached. When you approach your psychological state at any point in time with your emotions, you find that the emotions are always constantly interfering with it.

Your emotions are constantly in a state of fluctuation, just due to the nature of emotions themselves. They are always changing from person to person, and that is important to keep in mind. When you are well aware of the fact that your emotions will always be directly interacting with your mind and your behaviors.

Imagine that you were already feeling pretty annoyed as you got onto the road to drive home from work. You were already frustrated, and because of that, as you drove, when someone else cuts you off, you slam on your horn angrily. Angrily honking at the person, you try to pass them just to be done with it, but the other person interprets it as an attempt to race. They speed up to block you from crossing past them, and that was enough to make the situation worse.

At the end of the day, you almost get into an accident before swerving off of that main road and onto another street altogether, swearing and raging angrily. You then get home and are incredibly short with your children and partner, all because you are already in that combative mindset, and you end up upsetting the people who were simply happy to have you come home.

The Purpose of Emotions

Emotions themselves have two primary purposes—they allow for nonverbal communication, which is critical on its own, and they allow for the constant motivation to keep you alive. Effectively, your emotions exist because your unconscious mind needs a method through which to interact with the world around it.

Keeping in mind that the mind has two distinct parts, the conscious and unconscious, it is important to recognize that the two rarely, if ever, communicate with each other. They are unable to actively and reliably communicate between the two of them, and because of that, they are not always as effective as they could be.

The unconscious mind seeks to guide behavior—it takes care of anything throughout your day that does not require any attention, such as paying attention to what you need to do, how you need to do it, and making sure that you are able to do what

59

you need to do without wasting the space of your conscious mind.

Think for a moment about how your conscious mind is directly responsible for your perceptions and conscious decisions—it takes care of the heavy lifting and anything that does require attention. For example, take into consideration the act of writing an email—your conscious mind is able to decide exactly what you wish to write, while your unconscious mind takes care of the active typing that you do in order to put the point across appropriately. This means that your unconscious mind does the more menial of the tasks—paying attention to how you are typing and manually controlling your fingers, so you do not have to.

The unconscious mind is typically the quicker of the two simply because it is automatic. It happens without the conscious mind having the opportunity to influence it. You simply do what it is expecting you to do. Of course, you *can* consciously override it if you know what you are about to do, but for the most part, you are not going to see that happen.

Now, writing an email is relatively low-stakes—it does not matter much if you make a typo because all you need to do is correct it. However, imagine that we are considering a more dangerous situation. Perhaps you are driving down the road when a truck suddenly veers into your path in traffic. You slam on your brakes to avoid hitting them before you even realize what is happening—your unconscious mind was responsible.

Communication

At this point, it is time to look at emotions more in-depth in terms of a mode of communication. When you feel an emotion, your body naturally changes in response. You may feel yourself shrinking inward when you are nervous, hunching over and cursing your arms to protect yourself. You may find yourself actively attempting to avoid eye contact.

This directly tells everyone around you a very specific message—you are uncomfortable and closed off. Your own behaviors actively tell other people that you are trying to avoid interaction and that you wish to be left alone. This is your way of communicating nonverbally.

Nonverbal communication encompasses so much of the way that we communicate with other people. It takes into consideration body language, such as how close or far away from others you are willing to get, to how likely you are to make any concessions in how you approach someone else. What is particularly critical to remember is that when you are interacting with other people, you need to consider the fact that their body language is incredibly telling, and that is because their body language tells of their emotions.

Think for a moment about cognitive behavioral therapy. If you are not familiar with this therapy, it is a combination of cognitive therapy and behavioral therapy. It looks at the fact that thoughts influence emotions, emotions influence behaviors, and behaviors then reinforce thoughts. This means that if you can read the body language, you can analyze in order to identify the emotion being felt. If you can figure out which emotion is being felt at any given moment, you can then begin to figure out why that emotion is being felt in the first place, allowing you better access to the mind of others. This will allow you to gain valuable feedback that you otherwise would not have access to. When you understand the mindset of someone else, then you are better able to interact with the people. You can make it a point to behave in ways that you know are conducive to the behavior that you want because you know about this cycle of thoughts, feelings, and behavior, and you recognize that your own body language allows for communication back toward the other person.

Motivators

Now, let's look at your emotions as motivators—consider how, when you were in danger, driving on the road, you slammed on your brakes without being conscious of doing so. This is because, for that moment, in your extreme state of emotion, your unconscious mind took hold. It was able to guide you through the process of slamming on that brake to protect yourself because the unconscious mind is largely dedicated to keeping you alive and functional. You need to be able to protect yourself in order to stay alive.

Your emotions work when your unconscious mind feels the need to actively intervene in a process or attempt to do something. Effectively, the emotions are designed to skew you toward the behaviors that make the most sense for your own given situation. Think about how you would feel if someone continually harassed you at work—you would be angry. This is a direct response to not having your need for boundaries met. Your boundaries were repeatedly being crossed, and no matter how much you tried to tell the person kindly to leave you alone, you found that the boundary breeches kept happening over and over again, so you eventually gave up hope of getting through to the person and snapped at them. You were motivated by your anger to enforce your own boundaries that were being disregarded.

Each of your primary emotions serve a very specific motivational purpose—they guide you toward some sort of behavior set in order to make sure that your basic interpersonal needs are met. You are able to enforce that you need, for example, for someone to help you when you are afraid or sad. You communicate something clear: There is something wrong, and there may even potentially be some level of danger that must be given the proper consideration as well.

When you keep emotions as a motivator in mind, they start to become incredibly easy to understand. When you feel angry, you know that you are having some sort of boundary broken, and it is frustrating you. When you feel sad, you know it is because something is hurting you, and you feel the need to fight back against it or to get support, and so on.

However, in modern-day, many times, the situations that trigger our emotions do not line up so much with what used to say they were developed in nature. You may feel scared, but that fear is coming from a place of fearing losing something rather than a fear of death or otherwise being threatened. Effectively, you will react with fear to a situation that does not actually warrant such a strong reaction. For example, having someone comment something cruel on your social media page is different than feeling truly threatened by the situation at hand as if you were staring down the mouth of a cougar or some other animal that was primarily determined to eat and kill you.

This means that most of the time, your emotional impulses are usually gross overreactions to what they otherwise should have been. You do not need to react like someone is trying to kill you if they are simply telling you that they disagree with you, nor do you need to actively attack and fight to the death over some sort of misunderstanding or who gets that last pack of toilet paper at the grocery store.

Of course, that does not, by any means, mean that your emotions are unimportant or should not be considered. Your emotions are critical in several contexts, and being able to recognize your emotions can help you know exactly how you are feeling at any given moment. What is important, however, is knowing when to put that distance between yourself and what is happening, and when those emotional impulses developed over millennia of survival of the fittest in nature are actually appropriate to act upon.

The Cause of Emotions

Despite the attempts to explain the cause of emotions, ranging from the spirits and passions of old philosophical psychology all the way to assuming that it is some sort of hormonal event, the only constant between everyone's explanations of what causes emotions is that there is no definitive answer. In fact, there are six major theories on what causes people to have emotions in the first place and what triggers them. Within this section, we will address all six of these theories, allowing you to come up with your own explanation and theory upon hearing them. The six major theories of emotion are the Evolutionary Theory, the Cognitive Appraisal Theory, the Facial-Feedback Theory, the James-Lange Theory, the Cannon-Bard Theory, and the Schacter-Singer Theory.

Ultimately, these theories can be understood in three ways—as being physiological in nature, asserting that the body is what causes emotions, being neurological in theory, asserting that the brain is responsible for emotions, and being cognitive in theory, asserting that thoughts and mental states are influential over emotions.

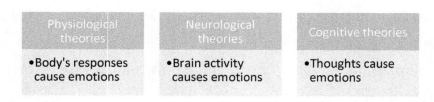

Evolutionary Theory

Starting off with Charles Darwin, the Evolutionary Theory states that emotions exist to keep animals capable of survival and reproduction. Effectively, we feel some positive emotions to lead toward mating, while other emotions encourage people to fight or run away. Ultimately, within this theory, emotions are adaptive—they are motivating and allow for quick responses to the environment.

Understanding how emotions work in others also allows for adaptive survival—when you are able to understand the feelings of others, you can effectively make sure that you are capable of protecting yourself. For example, if you know that feeling angry makes people volatile and prepared to fight back if the need arises, you may see someone showing defensive or aggressive behaviors and intentionally distance yourself from them. You will effectively ensure that you stay safe and comfortable because you are making it a point to avoid encouraging any behaviors that could become problematic for you. You are able to effectively respond because you understand the emotional signs of the other animal or person.

Cognitive Appraisal Theory

Within appraisal theories, it becomes clear that thinking must happen prior to an emotion occurring. Effectively, within a series of events that will trigger an emotion, the thought that happens after the stimulus is what determines the emotions. Think about how you may be absolutely terrified at the sight of a spider, but someone else is more than happy to walk around with their pet tarantula hanging out on their shoulder. The reason that you may be terrified by a spider that brings someone else great joy is the thought processes behind it.

The Facial-Feedback Theory

It has been noted over the years that sometimes, the body's responses do have a direct impact on emotions instead of being a consequence of that emotion. Some people take this to the extreme—they assume that it is the changes in the facial muscles, then, that caused emotions. Think about how if you have to smile at someone, eventually, you start actually having a better time than you otherwise would have. This is because you are engaging with your facial muscles and your facial muscles are directly responsible.

This may seem far-fetched to some, but consider that both Charles Darwin and William James, who you will hear more about momentarily, both recognized that link between physical and emotional. Because of backers by people like Darwin and James, people who believe in these theories, the facial-feedback theory did manage to become one of the more well-known.

James-Lange Theory

Of all, however, perhaps the best known theory of the cause of emotions is the James-Lange theory. In particular, this theory was developed by the psychologist, William James, and the physiologist Carl Lange. Together, the two pieced together a theory that stated that emotional responses are born from a result of physiological reactions to events.

This may seem complicated but consider for a moment what happens when you see a wolf or a bear or another predator staring you down from your yard. Most likely, you will feel your heart rate quicken. You will notice that your body seems to shake and run cold. Your breathing pattern changes. These physiological responses, then, must be interpreted somehow. After all, think about how similar several of those sensations are to extreme excitement as well? If you are extremely excited, you will also feel your heart rate and breathing increase.

The James-Lange theory says, then, that the only difference between your feeling of a racing heart being for excitement or for terror is how you think about it. You are essentially set to interpret your physiological response, and then that provides your emotion. Instead of feeling your heart race because you are scared, you feel scared because your heart is actively racing.

The Cannon-Bard Theory

Another common theory is known as the Cannon-Bard theory—and this one is set out to show disagreement with the James-Lange theory. Effectively, because it is entirely possible and expected that people will have physiological responses for various reasons, it is impossible to say that it is solely the physical that determines the emotional. Further, because emotional states are so rapid, it is impossible for them to be a result of physical changes. After all, we feel the emotion immediately with the symptoms—if the physical came first, then there would be a slight lag in the onset of the emotion and the physiological reaction.

In order to address these issues with the James-Lange theory of emotion, the Cannon-Bard theory was born. Within this theory, Cannon suggests that your emotions are a result of the thalamus within the brain to respond to some sort of stimulus. That one message gets sent out and triggers the emotional experience while also triggering the physiological at the same time. Effectively, the one message gets interpreted in two different ways.

For example, imagine that you walk out to your car, only to find a bear staring at you. Your body takes in the stimulus—you register visually being aware of the bear. Yoru thalamus then seeks to respond to the bear. In response, the message from the

70

thalamus makes you feel terrified, while simultaneously creating your sensations of fear—you feel shaky and nervous, for example. You feel your heart race. You want to run.

Schachter-Singer Theory

The final theory that we will address is the Schacter-Singer theory, also known commonly as the two-factor theory. This is a cognitive theory in which the physiological response must occur first prior to the creation of an emotion. In response to the physiological, then you must figure out why that arousal is happening and then label it yourself. Effectively, only then can you figure out the emotion.

This theory is quite similar to the Cannon-Bard and the James-Lange theories, drawing from both to create a new one to explain the working of emotions. Consider first how the James-Lange theory proposes that the emotions are based upon inferences from the physical reaction to a stimulus and how the Schachter-Singer theory mirrors that. Both the James-Lange and Schachter-Singer model point out that people make those inferences from physical to emotional, using a cognitive interpretation.

In regards to the Cannon-Bard theory, the two both agree that the same physical reaction can cause several different emotions. For example, you can acknowledge one particular sensation, such as trembling, as fear in one situation when you are staring down the bear, but sometimes, trembling can be a direct result of your own excitement for something.

So, if the Schachter-Singer model involves a physical response being cognitively interpreted, imagine that you have just walked outside, and that bear is sitting there, staring at you. You notice that you start to shake and that your heart is pounding. You look at the bear and acknowledge that the bear's presence is what is causing you to feel these signs of arousal—you are hyper-aware of the bear's presence. You must then understand what the sight of the bear means—you acknowledge and recognize that the bear's presence would be deemed to be a threat, and you respond accordingly. You acknowledge that the bear's presence is a threat and that the threat should be met with feelings of fear. Thus, you determine that the trembling and racing heart that you felt in response to seeing the bear is fear.

The Universal Emotions

Along with all of the ways that emotions could possibly be caused, another common point to contend with is whether emotions are universal. It is currently believed that emotions that you feel, from being pleasantly surprised, to moderately irritated, to even feeling guilty, all come from what are known as the seven universal emotions. These seven emotions are sort of families for others and many of the emotions that people know and recognize come as a series of several of these emotions. The seven universal emotions are anger, contempt, disgust, fear, joy, sadness, and surprise. Any other emotions exist somewhere on the spectrum within those confines.

Each of these seven emotions convey very important messages for those present around them. They convey some sort of need that is unmet, or in the case of happiness, a lack of unmet needs altogether. Understanding the needs that these emotions convey aids dramatically in the managing of relationships with others. These emotions are determined to be universal because they are recognizable, no matter where the individual that is exposed to them is from. They are effectively a way to communicate that seems to be innate—in fact, even people who have grown up blind still convey body language related to these seven emotions.

Anger

Anger as an emotion is strongly motivational. It is a response that is incredibly intense and is meant to be used as a response to perceiving a threat of some sort. When you experience anger, you are usually conveying to other people that you are feeling threatened—you are saying that you have a need for defense or boundaries.

Contempt

Contempt is incredibly close to anger—it is a feeling that whatever you are looking at or dealing with is beneath you to some degree. You show that it is worthless to you effectively. It is to treat other people or a thing with disregard or disdain—effectively, you are saying that you do not respect that other person or what that other person is doing. This is showing a need for space from the other person—you are effectively disgusted by the presence of that other person.

Disgust

Disgust is that feeling you get when you look at something repulsive. If you have ever smelled a foul diaper or opened a pack of food only to find that it is covered in mold, you have probably experienced disgust to some degree. When you feel disgust toward something, you are feeling an intense need to get away from something—likely because it poses a threat to your health and safety. You feel disgust to keep you from eating something moldy or toxic; for example—the smell or look is enough to sort of turn your stomach and discourage you from continuing.

Fear

Fear is the feeling you get when you are exposed to something that is a significant threat to you—it leads to either the fight or flight response, and as a response, you either feel afraid, which will cause you to flee, or your fear shifts over to anger instead and you move into the fight response. Fear is a necessary emotion to keep you safe—it encourages you to defend yourself by conveying a need to protect or defend. It tells other people that you have a need for safety that you need help meeting.

Joy

Joy is the state of feeling happy or calm with what is happening. You feel comfortable in your surroundings, and you are content with what is going on, or you are even enjoying yourself and what is happening. When you are experiencing joy, you are experiencing a lack of needs. All of your needs have been met, and you are enjoying yourself.

Sadness

Sadness is felt for a very important reason—it is meant to be adaptive. Sadness has very real purposes that are integral for a happy life, as contradictory as it seems. It reminds you to pay attention to what brings meaning to your life. It tells you that you should appreciate what you have. It allows you to feel centered and grounded and also encourages resilience. It shows that you have a need for support, and it reminds people to provide that help and resilience for you.

Surprise

Finally, surprise brings with it the need to pay attention to something. It shows some sort of disconnect between your expectations and what you had in front of you. You may have expected one thing, only to find that your expectations were entirely avoided altogether. Effectively, then, you feel the need to pay closer attention to whatever is happening around you to figure out what is going on with it. This also signals to others as well to pay closer attention as whatever is happening is deviating from the expected.

Emotions, Moods, and Feelings

Finally, as we wrap up this chapter, it is time to pay special attention to the difference between emotions, feelings, and moods. Despite the fact that we may refer to all three of them as the same thing, they are all distinctly different from each other. Your feelings and emotions are different, as are your moods. While they are closely related to each other, you must be able to recognize the inherent differences as well, especially considering that they become quite relevant to understand later on.

Overall, however, the primary difference is time. Time take something from an emotion to a feeling and from a feeling to a mood. Effectively, the three work together with similar sensations, but they do have differing purposes.

Emotions are believed to be the chemical response to the trigger and is nearly instantaneous. The brain is able to understand the stimulus and trigger the chemicals necessary within about half a second. These chemicals go throughout the body, which is why many of your emotions also directly impact your body as well. These emotions last for roughly six seconds before the initial emotion fades.

Feelings, then, are the integration of the emotion. We understand the emotion that was felt and begin to understand it. We feel both physically, such as when you dip your foot in hot water and feel that it is hot, and we feel emotionally as well, such as in response to a strong emotion. As opposed to the emotions, which were pushed forward by the brain and chemicals, feelings are cognitive. They are usually several emotions coming together, along with the thoughts surrounding. They are also longer-lasting, but still not permanent.

Finally, **moods** are general sensations. They are your general state at any given time. When you are in a good mood, then you are feeling mostly good about yourself and what is happening. You are generally calm and relaxed, for example, and you are likely to be more patient. When you are in a bad mood, on the other hand, you may find that you have no patience whatsoever to deal with anything.

Chapter 5: Managing Thoughts and Regulating Emotions

Imagine that you were heading through the grocery store to pick up some last-minute items before you go home for dinner. It is the Friday before the following Thanksgiving, and you know that the store will be packed. You have already had a bad day and were already feeling impatient. Let's really set the stage here— you have two sick children at home, and your third child just got suspended. Your car died earlier in the day and you are overall just at the end of your rope. You cannot put up with anything else going wrong.

Of course, however, despite feeling like you cannot deal with anything else, you find out that 2/3 things that you went to the store for are , in fact, sold out, and you cannot get them. You needed them for your big holiday dinner, and without them, you cannot possibly finish the meal. Perhaps it was the big main dish that is missing—perhaps there is no turkey left to buy. You lose it right there. You yell at the attendant who had just asked if there is anything that you needed. You tell him that you are furious that they do not have any turkeys when it is Thanksgiving, and you cannot believe that the store dropped the ball so badly. You completely unload on this poor, 16-year-old grocery store shelf stocker who does nothing but make sure that there is food on the shelves.

In reality, it is not the employee's fault—he is not the one responsible for the lack of turkeys. Sure, the store could have ordered more, but in reality, the only one to blame for the lack of turkey at that point is you. You could have gone earlier in the week to get one, which would have made much more sense. You could have tried going to another store to get one, but you were too tired to continue driving around everywhere. You could have done plenty of different things, but at the end of the day, you chose instead to yell at a poor teenaged employee who probably had better things to be doing at that point in time.

In this example, it is a sign of struggling with emotional regulation. It is okay to feel furious at your situation, but what is not acceptable is deciding to take it out on some random, innocent person who had nothing to do with what you were feeling. As much as it can make you feel better to yell at someone else, it is not particularly healthy to do so. It is not fair to the employee that you yelled at, nor is it a solid method of managing your own emotions.

Being able to self-regulate is a critical skill for everyone to learn—adults and children alike. When you can self-regulate, you can keep yourself from responding negatively, such as in the instance above. You know how to deal with your emotions and allow them to be felt in a manner that is healthy and actually conducive to solving the problem. Instead of screaming, you could have chosen to go to another store, for example, or asked when they are getting more turkey in, rather than risking getting permanently banned.

Of course, there is more to self-regulation than just managing emotions, as well—you can also manage your thoughts to manage yourself as well. When you are able to manage your thoughts, you are able to regulate yourself as well. Think back to how your own thoughts could alter how you register your emotions—if you feel like your emotions are going to be skewed by your thoughts, you may need to change the thought to ensure that it does not happen. For example, you may want to manage your thoughts surrounding your current phobia in order to avoid your emotions from being problematic.

As we go over this chapter, you will be learning about several situations in which you may need to manage your thoughts. You will learn about negative thoughts and cognitive distortions and how these thoughts need to be mitigated due to their tendency to have negative impacts on your emotional state. You will learn about how to manage thoughts, looking at using both cognitive behavioral therapy and emotional intelligence to help you do so. You will then focus specifically on emotional regulation, understanding what it entails and why it should happen. Finally, as this chapter comes to a close, you will look at several techniques that are used to manage thoughts and regulate emotions.

By the time that you have finished this chapter, you should feel comfortable with the idea of regulating both your emotions and your thoughts. In doing so, you will find that there is a positive impact on your life. You will feel more capable of handling yourself in difficult or negative situations. You will feel more in control of yourself, and you will find that even your most strained relationships of the past will actually become more easily managed.

When Thoughts Require Management

Have you ever had a thought, and then moments later wished that you had not had a thought like it? Perhaps you had a thought that triggered you to act, such as the example in the grocery store, in which you were so overwhelmed with your day that you lashed out emotionally at everyone present. After the fact, as you sat in your car and gathered your thoughts, you may have felt embarrassed or like you wish you had managed the situation much better than before.

We all have thoughts from time to time that are problematic. You may get down on yourself for messing up something that you thought was extra important, such as telling yourself that you are useless for failing. You may find that you were stuck thinking in what you will soon come to recognize as a cognitive distortion—thinking that is illogical and problematic and therefore should be disregarded.

While it is normal to have these thoughts from time to time, it is critical to make sure that you are able to recognize them so they can be corrected. You need to be able to regulate, reminding yourself that these thoughts that you are having are not conducive to being happy or successful, and for that reason, you should disregard them. This section seeks to identify both negative thoughts and negative emotions, so you know how to handle yourself. In learning to do so, you can counter them before they can get out of hand once and for all.

Negative thoughts

Have you ever walked into a situation while immediately wondering what will happen if you fail? Perhaps you talk yourself out of trying to do something because you are convinced that your attempt will always be a failure. No matter how much you try to convince yourself otherwise, you get caught up in the thoughts of negativity—your thoughts are rooted in can'ts and won'ts, and despite even acknowledging that your current thinking is far too negative, you cannot help but continue on.

Ultimately, negative thinking is any thinking that is inherently locked into functioning form a place of fear. It is negative and dangerous, and no matter what you attempt to do to erase it, you find that it keeps coming back. The apprehension that you feel that drives these thoughts directly challenges you—it keeps you back, convincing you that you cannot actually get through the processes that you need. It makes you feel like you are worthless, leaving you to feel guilty because you believe that you are incapable, while simultaneously feeling guilty for never trying in the first place.

These negative thoughts are largely contagious—they can be based on what should be or what must be, effectively creating some sort of obligation. You should be able to do that, or you must make sure that you finish that work before the deadline, and if you are unable to do so, then there is a problem. This sort of logic is problematic—it sort of forces you into this impossible situation in which you think you have to do something a certain way, and anything beyond that certain way is failing. When you are caught up in negative thoughts, you find that you repeat them over and over again. You have a thought, which causes guilt, which causes inaction, which reinforces the thought, causing further guilt.

Most often, these occur because of a fear of some sort. You may be afraid of failing or afraid of venturing into unknown territory if you are entirely unfamiliar with the situation that you are entering. This causes problems, especially as the thoughts become automatic and repeated without effort. This leads you to sort of attempt to do better, but really get caught up in inaction instead, creating the aforementioned cycle.

Cognitive Distortions

Those negative thoughts mentioned are just one form of cognitive distortions. Cognitive distortions themselves refer to any sort of exaggerated thought pattern that is frequently quite irrational. In being irrational, you often see problems related to them. You may have a thought about how things must o a certain way, and when they do not, you struggle to compensate. Alternatively, you may think in another way that leads you to feel like you understand exactly what is going through the mind of the person you are attempting to interact with. You assume that you know, even though you have no true way to do so. These sorts of thoughts are known as cognitive distortions, and oftentimes, if a thought falls into any of the distortions that are being listed here, you know that you can disregard them altogether.

To better understand this, think of proper logic. There are several forms of logic, known as fallacies, that are simply inaccurate. They cannot possibly be used because they simply do not make sense in formal logic. No matter how hard you may attempt to justify something in logic with a fallacy, it will still never be any more valid as a form of argument. The cognitive distortions that you are likely to encounter at any point in time are:

- **The need to always be right:** This thinking assumes that it is impossible to be wrong. Effectively, when you fall for this thought process, you try to justify your own thoughts and feelings at all costs, looking for literally any way that you can possibly force what you have asserted as being true, even if it involves you looking strange as you do it.

- **Casting blame:** When you use this distortion, you find that everyone else is held responsible for what they do wrong, and you are quick to remind them of this. You effectively always fault other people, even when, in reality, you would not push the idea so much.

- **Ignoring positivity:** When you use this distortion, you are effectively completely disregarding anything positive that occurs. Even if something good happened to you in the course of a day, you would sooner focus on how everything that day went wrong.

- **Emotional reasoning:** This particular form of reasoning is incredibly problematic. When you engage in emotional reasoning, you effectively allow your own emotional states to determine your thoughts on something. If you feel happy about something, you assume that it is positive, even if it is not necessarily the right choice for you. This is the sort of logic that lands you with a car payment you are struggling to afford simply because the thought of driving the car felt good, so you chose to get it.

- **Change fallacy:** With this distortion, you find that you rely on social control to get other people to cooperate. Effectively, you try to browbeat people into doing what you want or need, using pressure or other techniques to do so.

- **Fairness fallacy:** When you fall into this distortion, you are often making the assumption that things must be fair at all costs, and if they are not, you feel like something was unfair and, therefore, wrong. You feel like life, in general, should be fair, despite the fact that life is inherently unfair, and you then use your emotions about the unfairness of the situation as your reasoning for how you have behaved

- **Jumping to conclusions**: When you do this, you usually arrive at some sort of conclusion with absolutely no support for that thought process. Typically, it involves one of two forms of jumping to conclusions. You may engage in mind reading in which you assume that you know what the other party is thinking. You assume that their thoughts are negative, even when they may not be. This leads to you behaving according to how you assume the other people will, which can be a big problem if you are assuming that the other party is intentionally being negative or problematic. The other form of jumping to conclusions involves fortune-telling—when you are fortune-telling, you assume that you know how something will play out. You assume that the ending will be negative and act accordingly.

- **Labeling**: When you label someone, you are overgeneralizing—you effectively assume that someone's actions are directly indicative of someone's character. For example, if someone accidentally made a mistake, you may assume that they are generally quite incompetent and leave it at that.

- **Minimizing**: When you are minimizing something, you are intentionally downplaying it—you are trying to make it sound like it is less negative or problematic than it actually is. For example, you may tell yourself that whatever you have done well is not actually as good or beneficial to you as you thought it was initially.

- **Catastrophizing**: Sometimes, you go the opposite direction from minimizing—when you catastrophize, instead of making something smaller, you magnify it into something far worse than it actually is. You effectively make the situation out to be as terrible as possible.

- **Overgeneralization**: when you engage in this distortion, you find that you are making decisions and generalization without enough evidence one way or the other. You may assume that if your friend cancels plans with you due to life reasons, they do not like you, or they wish that you would stop inviting or taking them places.

- **Personalization**: When you personalize, you take everything personal. You allow yourself to be responsible for everything, whether good or bad, even if realistically, you had no true control or influence over what has happened.

- **Must statements**: When you do this, you focus on what must or should—this is expecting things to be different instead of attempting to change or better accommodate for what has happened.

- **Dichotomous thinking**: Finally, when you use dichotomous thinking, you think that everything is in extremes. It is either perfect or a failure. It is either always or never. When you do this, you fail to acknowledge all of the colors of grey that lay between the extremes.

Managing Thoughts

If you believe that your mind may be run by these negative sorts of thoughts, it may be important to begin to manage them. If you are able to manage your own thoughts, you can begin to manage your behaviors as well, and that is incredibly important most of the time. If you could have managed your emotions, you never would have blown up at the grocery store employee, for example—you would have accepted what had happened and moved on instead.

Managing thoughts can keep you calm when you are in the face of stress. It can make you more reliable and capable of protecting yourself. When you are able to manage your thoughts, you ensure that you are able to make the best in nearly any situation. Making the best of the situation is sometimes the best that you can do, and without it, you may feel weighed down upon or otherwise incapable. This is why managing your thoughts can be so incredibly beneficial.

Ultimately, there are several methods through which you can manage the thoughts of others. The two that will be focused upon, however, are managing through emotional intelligence and managing through cognitive restructuring, a common technique used within cognitive-behavioral therapy.

Managing thoughts with CBT

Cognitive restructuring is a common exercise within CBT—it is done in order to identify any problematic thoughts that you have, such as your negative thoughts or cognitive distortions, and then find some sort of method that you can use to tackle them. Usually, the technique is designed to override through constant thought challenging or otherwise making oneself into an unreliable judge of the situation at hand.

For example, imagine that you are terrified of finding help form other people. Just the act of having to ask someone else for help is enough to leave you absolutely terrified. When this happens, you will find that even asking for help in an emergency is nearly impossible. You struggle to ever actively address those that may be in a position to help you, and because of that, you are failing far more than you should be.

Of course, this fear of asking for help leads to constant failure. You do not ask, and then as a natural consequence, you fail. This is problematic—you cannot get through life constantly failing. For that reason, you decide that you will use cognitive restructuring to help defend yourself. You then focus on identifying the thoughts responsible for that fear of asking for help so you can directly target them. You may make it a point to tell yourself that your thought process is flawed because it hits the distortion list, for example, and therefore, it does not matter. It may involve other methods such as constant reinforcement through constant repetition, effectively drilling the thought into the mind of someone else. No matter the method that you use, what holds true is that you should be able to change the thoughts that you have in order to protect yourself in the future.

Managing thoughts with emotional intelligence

Compared to cognitive behavioral therapy, the methods of thought control within emotional intelligence may seem a bit vaguer and less intuitive. In particular, you will find that when you must fix your negative thoughts with emotional intelligence, you are actively making it a point to prevent them from happening in the first place. You may use methods such as affirmations and cognitive restructuring, or you may find that you are better off with other methods instead to best defend yourself.

When you use emotional intelligence to regulate your thoughts, you are effectively making sure that your thoughts are healthy by learning to bypass the negative ones. Yes, the negative thoughts must be defeated in any way possible. However, you must also keep in mind that it is incredibly important for you to make it a point to defend against them as well.

Emotional intelligence is so incredibly effective with these forms of thought because of the fact that emotional intelligence teaches discipline and control. When you are learning to be emotionally intelligent, you are learning to be resilient, capable of any change that comes your way, and more. You effectively figure out how best to get around poor or negative emotions by learning to recognize that, as negative thoughts, they deserve no more consideration than they have already had by the time they have been acknowledged in the first place. You are able to remind yourself that you should not, in fact, give in to your every whim and thought, and instead make sure that you are able to see past the impulses and toward the goals that you have set out for yourself.

Emotional Regulation

Emotional regulation occurs largely the same way no matter which method you choose—emotional intelligence or cognitive behavioral therapy. However, what is important to note is that when you choose to use emotional regulation, you are not completely disregarding the emotions that you are having at any given moment. Remember, feeling emotions is incredibly important and incredibly powerful. Rather than not feeling emotions, you focus on how to regulate—you are making it a point to learn how best to target your feelings and ensure that they do not get in your way rather than telling yourself that what you are feeling is wrong.

For example, imagine that you are upset at the grocery store all over again. It is okay to be upset—what was not okay was effectively blowing up on someone who was entirely unrelated to the person that was there with you. Rather than moving on like nothing important went wrong, you are choosing to acknowledge that a problem has occurred, and then you are better able to begin to figure out how to control the emotions that caused it in the first place.

A

Perhaps the better name for this is to build up emotional tolerance—when you are engaging in emotional regulation, you continue to feel all of the major emotions. The only difference is that you have learned to be mindful—you have learned to be conscientious of the entire concept having to avoid emotions at all. Instead, you allow those emotions to be felt and learn from them. There is always something more that you can learn from someone or a situation if you really look for it.

Managing your Thoughts and Feelings

When you are ready to manage your thoughts, one method that is commonly used is through affirmations. In particular, you make it clear that you can manage your thoughts by repeating positive thoughts to yourself until you internalize and believe them. For example, imagine that you have just been told that you are fired due to not stocking enough turkeys—if you are able to manage your thoughts, you can keep yourself from spiraling into a depression in which you blame yourself endlessly. Instead of seeing the situation as your own fault, you are able to figure out what to do next.

Affirmations

Affirmations refer to the short statements that you will reiterate to yourself on a regular basis. You will use these affirmations whenever you feel like you are struggling in any way. For example, if you find that you cannot manage to get over a negative thought about your own worthlessness, you can come up with an affirmation that will help you directly counter it. All that you have to do is make sure that you are able to come up with an affirmation that is formed well enough to help you do so. Using affirmations is incredibly important to regulating your negative feelings, helping you to overcome them in order to keep moving forward.

When you are making affirmations, it hopes to remember three distinct rules—keep it personal, keep it positive, and keep it present-oriented. If you can remember these three rules, you will find that even the most difficult and stubborn of negative thoughts can ultimately be slain like the monster it is.

Present   Positive   Personal

You must keep your affirmation personal because ultimately, at the end of the day, literally, the only person and situation that you have the utmost control over is yourself. When you are not the subject of the affirmation, you will find that you cannot act upon it, meaning that you cannot possibly ensure that the affirmation will be true at the end of the day, rendering it almost ineffective in the first place.

You must make sure that your affirmation is positive—when it is not, you are hardly helping yourself defeat a negative thought. While a negative times a negative in multiplication may create a positive, that is not the case in real-world interactions. If you have just been cut off while driving to work, the right answer is not to tailgate the other party and harass them until the police arrive. This means that if you wish to be effective, you want to make sure that your affirmation is positive.

Finally, your affirmation must be present-oriented. This means that it is actively true at the exact moment that it is being discussed. You must be able to acknowledge the truthfulness of the affirmation if you hope to use it for cognitive restructuring.

When these three rules come together, you effectively create an affirmation that is actionable because it is present-tense and able to tackle a very specific problem that you may have. When they come together, you can find that you are more than capable of ensuring that you are encouraging a good state of mind because you are using positive language. Finally, you know that it is focused specifically on you, so you know that the thought that you are correcting is well within your own jurisdiction.

Cognitive Restructuring

Another common method to regulate is through cognitive restructuring. This process primarily involves four steps—you must identify the problematic thoughts, you must identify any distortions, you must dispute the distortions, and then you must develop an argument to the negative thoughts. If you follow these four steps, you can eventually overcome the negative thoughts or distortions that are present.

Identify automatic thought → Identify cognitive distortions → Dispute cognitive distortion → Develop a new thought

By starting with identifying, you know exactly what you will be targeting, and because of that, you know where your efforts are going. In figuring these out, you are identifying either negative thoughts or cognitive distortions that will be challenged.

By identifying any of the distortions that exist, you already sort of put a chip in their armor. After all, if you know that something about the thoughts is inherently flawed, you will be able to actively protest against that thought process. You may be able to remind yourself of the problems in order to better overcome it, for example. You will be able to recognize that there is an inherent flaw that can help you throw out the thought altogether. After all, if someone came up and told you that, in their country, 2+2=6, you would look at them like they are crazy. It is the hope that, through recognizing distortions, you would give that same look to your distorted thoughts.

Next, it is time to dispute the automatic thoughts. You may do this through actively questioning yourself and your thoughts, such as wondering how those particular thoughts are truthful or wondering why you would follow that particular train of logic in the first place.

Finally, in developing a rational rebuttal, you are coming up with a new way of thinking. You are replacing the old thought with a new one here, offering up an alternative thought that actually makes sense. You may tell yourself that instead of feeling like you are worthless and then telling yourself that you are worthless, which is effectively just thinking with emotional reasoning and following it up with some degree of labeling as well, you tell yourself that you are trying the best that you can.

Emotional Regulation

Ultimately, grounding yourself is a technique that is largely personal. What works for you may not necessarily work for others as well, but what is important is that you are willing to try to see what does, in fact, work for you. You may find that you do best with some sort of mindfulness technique in order to regulate your emotions. You may feel like you need a breathing exercise or some other exercise altogether. What is the most important during this time is that you are choosing a method that feels comfortable for you. Ultimately, you must be comfortable enough to use these methods during moments of extreme duress in certain situations. For this reason, it is always recommended that you use these grounding methods several times before ever actually needing them. You want to ensure that you have practiced enough to ensure that you are actually capable of using them when they matter most.

Grounding Method

One such manner of grounding yourself involves the use of your surroundings. When you use this manner, you are effectively making sure that you can focus on everything around you, identifying and engaging with your senses in order to make sure that you are focused on what is around you rather than what you are doing.

In this instance, you will engage each of your senses one at a time in order to sort of bring yourself down from the emotional state. Think of this as slowly making your way back to shore after going out too far into the middle of the lake.

Starting with your vision, find five things around you that you can see. Make a note of each one as you do so. Then, move on to four things that you can hear around you. Third, you want to identify three things that you can touch. Fourth, you must be able to identify two things that you can smell. Finally, you need one more thing that you can taste.

This serves two purposes—it distracts your mind by giving it something structured to look at and consider, and it also makes sure that you are able to regulate yourself. You effectively distract your mind from any sort of panic attack or troubles that you were having by using your senses as much as you can.

Deep Breathing

There is something oddly therapeutic about deep breathing—whatever it is; it makes it far easier for individuals to engage in changing their emotions. When you are using deep breathing, you are effectively activating the vagus nerve—a nerve that connects from the gut to the brain and is heavily involved in much of the physical and emotional connections.

When you use deep breathing, your deep breaths unintentionally activate the vagus nerve. This is not problematic for the vast majority, and actually making use of this nerve is actually quite healthy. Many cultures push a strong emphasis on this sort of method—they actively encourage you to use deep breathing, such as in prayers that naturally follow the rhythm of the vagus nerve, or in meditation that uses long, drawn-out sounds.

When you want to use deep breathing for emotional regulation, you effectively want to focus strongly on your breaths. Take in a deep breath, making the inhale last four seconds. As you do this, you want to count slowly. Hold your breath for four seconds as well before exhaling deeply through your mouth. When you do this, you are going to begin to feel the results quickly.

This method is incredibly effective. It allows you to actively remind your body that you are safe and that your emotional state should not be nearly as volatile as it appears to be during these moments of stress.

Chapter 6: Principles of Psychology and Your Relationships

Relationships are often considered critical to humankind. Though many people tell you that you should live life without allowing someone else to define it, nearly everyone is going to naturally crave a relationship of some sort. As a social species, you are commonly going to be exposed to people and commonly desire to fit in with them as well—this is only natural. When you feel these urges, it can be easy to remind yourself that you do not need to be worrying about a relationship or that you have no interest in a relationship. However, the vast majority of the time, this is not true.

You naturally want to have other people to spend your time with. You naturally want to ensure that you can relate to others, engaging with them, and living your life as happily as you possibly can. For this reason, it becomes important to understand the psychology behind the relationships that you will have. When you understand how they work psychologically, you will begin to figure out where any past relationships failed. If you have commonly run into relationships that fail, you may feel entirely discouraged from continuing to try to engage with them. However, if you were to engage in your relationships with a different mindset and attempt to approach them in the first place, you would find that you are actually far better off. You will find that your relationships will be happier and more successful, and this means that you, yourself, will be happier as well.

The Psychology of Relationships

You may be wondering why these relationships are so important to you in the first place—there is one particular reason for this: It is a basic human need. If you were to look at Maslow's hierarchy of needs, you would see love and belongingness right on the list, and this is because it is a proposed psychological need. No matter how much you may attempt to convince yourself otherwise, you feel a biological need to fit in and find love. You will keep searching for this as much as possible as well.

Romantic love, then, becomes one of the most important relationships that you have in life—in fact, you may find that your entire life is based upon finding such a relationship. This may seem absurd, but think about it—you spent time going to school so you could get a good job. You spent time working that job so you could save money for a house. You bought that house, so you had the time and space to have a family.

Effectively, when the biological imperative in life is to reproduce, you are going to be seeking out a mate. After all, you cannot reproduce on your own—you need a partner to do so. This means that your entire life is going to be a build-up to your romantic relationships.

Unfortunately, relationships have a tendency to fail. In failing, they also cause a great deal of sadness or frustration as a direct consequence. This makes sense—if your entire purpose in life is to reproduce, if you feel like you cannot have children because you cannot find a relationship, you are going to feel like you are failing, and that sense of failure can be debilitating. For this reason, learning to ensure that you have the skills to manage your relationships is critical. You need to know that you can manage your relationships as successfully as possible if you hope to ever actually keep and maintain a relationship.

Healthy Relationships

When you seek to build a healthy relationship, you may find that you have some serious soul-searching to do. Are you the one that is causing problems in the relationships? Is there something wrong with your own approach? In being willing and able to question the relationship from the perspective of others, you may find that you are actually doing several things that may make your relationship far more difficult to manage than you had intended.

Nevertheless, let's take a look at what a healthy relationship will typically look like. Understanding it can really help you gain insight into how best to approach your future relationships.

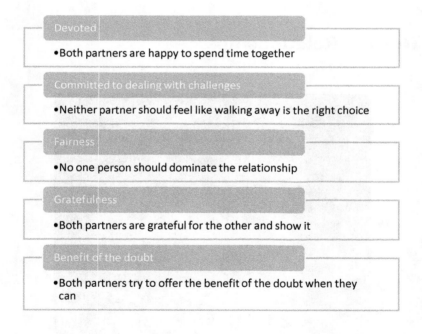

Devoted
•Both partners are happy to spend time together

Committed to dealing with challenges
•Neither partner should feel like walking away is the right choice

Fairness
•No one person should dominate the relationship

Gratefulness
•Both partners are grateful for the other and show it

Benefit of the doubt
•Both partners try to offer the benefit of the doubt when they can

First and foremost—you should always feel like you can communicate with your partner. When you are able to communicate effectively with your partner, you and your partner can work through almost any problem together. Effectively, working together creates a situation in which you can actively engage together, understanding both sides of the problems until you can both come to some sort of consensus or solution.

Beyond that, both parties should be willing to spend time together. You should trust that your partner *wants* to spend time with you, and even if that time is difficult to find in the first place, it is critical for you to find it if you hope to be effective in your relationships. You must also be willing to accommodate when challenges arise. Perhaps your partner has to go away for two weeks for work—will you be okay? Some weaker relationships may struggle with this, but if you are able to cope with it, you may find that distance makes the heart fonder.

Your relationship should also be quite fair—both parties should put in a reasonable amount of work. Remember one critical aspect here—fair is not always equal. If one party works an inordinate amount of time, then it is only fair to assume that the other party is going to be doing more of the housework. For example, say that you work a standard 40-hour workweek, and your partner works regular 60 hour work weeks. Since you are home 50% more than your partner, it makes sense that you would take a larger amount of the housework. This does not mean that your partner would be exempt, but you would not have to do nearly as much.

All of the above leads to a relationship based upon gratefulness for each other, and both partners are willing to show it. Further, you and your partner are then both far more willing to provide that sense of camaraderie and love that you have been seeking. When you are able to maintain that camaraderie long-term, you will strengthen your relationship.

Reciprocity and Relationships

Reciprocity is critical in nearly every context in your personal and social life. Because reciprocity is one of those things in which you do it, or you do not, when you are always willing to include reciprocity with your relationships, you are able to better the relationship in general. Reciprocity refers to how likely you are to return the favor.

Within intimate relationships, reciprocity is critical. It is the epitome of equality—both you and your partner feel like neither of you are willing to put up with the idea that one of you would be dominant in the relationship. This does not mean dominant in the sense that one member of the relationship tends to care more than the other about trivial matters such as where you are going out to eat or what you will do on date night—it refers to dominance in the sense of utter control. While some relationships can make this work, for the most part, a relationship in which one party is able to entirely dominate and control the entire thing is not usually considered particularly relationship friendly.

Reciprocity in a relationship implies that you and your partner are willing to cooperate, as well as recognizing the idea that while you and your partner are individual people with your own likes and dislikes, you are also people that are highly interdependent. You rely upon each other and are committed to nurturing those feelings toward each other.

With that in mind, you may begin to see why reciprocity is so important. This is not referring simply to reciprocity in the sense that you must be returning a gift at the next gift-giving season after one person has given a gift to the other—rather, this sort of reciprocity occurs when the two of you have dedicated yourselves to ensuring that the other is taken care of. It is the idea of being willing to offer to scratch your partner's back before your partner asks you to, and then getting your own back scratched in return.

Please note, however, that the expectation of reciprocity can sometimes lead to some serious disconnects. Remember that in your relationships, you should not be expecting anything. Expecting that leads to your own entitlement, which is the exact opposite of reciprocity.

Commitments and Relationships

Next, keep in mind that commitments are critical in relationships. If you are making a commitment within your relationship, you are offering to do a certain set of things for the other person, and this should not be taken lightly. When you take this sort of behavior lightly, you may find that you actually struggle to find people with whom you can create a meaningful relationship. After all, commitments can be scary and difficult to make, especially early on. However, people value commitment, and if you are afraid to commit, you are essentially afraid to ever have a functioning relationship as being willing and able to commit is perhaps one of the largest criteria for most people. If someone is not willing to commit to monogamy, most people are likely to struggle with the idea of the relationship in the first place. If you refuse to acknowledge that you will no longer pursue other people, the person you are actively dating is likely to dump you because you are effectively treating him as a backup in case someone else that catches the other person's fancy comes in.

When you are willing to commit to a relationship, however, you may notice that things are actually going to change for the better. If you are willing to make commitments, other people will be more willing to commit to you simply due to the idea that you should reciprocate when someone else does something for you.

This means then that in your relationships, you are likely to find someone somewhere that can, in fact, make things work the way that you want. When you do find them, as soon as you can get a commitment from them, you are likely to get whatever was committed.

Expectations and Relationships

Finally, one thing that is important to look at is what will happen when things expectations are added to a relationship. Expectations are certain things that you assume are going to happen simply because you believe it. In many instances, it is accurate, but today, he is wrong. When you are in a relationship with someone else, you may find that over time, it becomes incredibly easy to develop an expectation for that person.

When you are in a relationship with someone who does not tend to recognize reality for what it is, you may be working under a narcissist. In particular, when you look at a relationship that you have had in the past, can you identify any problematic behaviors that may have happened before. What was the root cause? Can you identify any of the times during that last relationship that you may have had some unrealistic expectations?

In particular, unrealistic expectations are amongst some of the worst that you can expose your partner too. If you have an unrealistic expectation that your partner should be a certain body type at all times, and you got with someone with that body type that eventually changed, if you left that relationship because it no longer met your expectation, you might have been unrealistic. Being unrealistic is typically quite bad—while it is important to have an idea of what you want, having several unrealistic standards can leave you scrambling to find a relationship with little to no luck. You may desperately try, and yet, at every turn, you find that people run away like their pants are on fire. This is a huge red flag that something you are doing is inappropriate or problematic.

With your relationships, perhaps the best thing that you can do is ensure that your expectations are reasonable. Ask yourself if you are willing to follow the expectations that you set out for yourself, for example. However, as you do this, remember that just because you are willing to do something does not mean that everyone is willing to do it, and you must keep that in mind. It is incredibly important for you to figure out what you absolutely want and need, while also juggling what is realistic and fair to expect out of the other party. You do not want to have these unrealistic expectations that are impossible to ever actually meet, as that is asking far too much out of the other party—that is not fair to them and should never be forced.

Chapter 7: The Psychology of Success

Success—everyone wants it. Whether you want a successful relationship, a successful career, or a successful life, you are striving for excellence, and that is okay. When you are striving for this sort of excellence, you are telling yourself that you deserve the best of what you have to offer yourself, and that is showing that you truly care about how you see yourself and what you do with yourself.

This is good—you are showing what you are deserving of. You are showing that you know that you deserve the best and that you are willing to put your best foot forward. However, you may feel like it is difficult to get past that point. What is success? How do you become successful? How can you be sure that you ultimately get the life that you feel that you deserve? This chapter seeks to help you answer these questions—we will come up with a definition of success .then, we will discuss how success exists as a psychology within emotional intelligence—and finally, how to strengthen emotional intelligence in order to ensure that you are as successful as you have set out to become.

When you are successful, one thing is for sure—you are opening up dozens of doors for yourself, and in doing so, you are bound to find one that is perfect for you. You will find one that serves you well and keeps you happy. It is simply a matter of finding happiness and figuring out how best to pursue it.

Making Your Own Definition of Success

Success is one of those things that is incredibly personal. Your own definition of success is likely to vary greatly from the definitions of those around you. This is okay—success is something that is entirely for you, so it is okay for it to be personal and varying based on the individual. You should make sure that the definition of success that you create is one that truly encompasses what you want to achieve.

In particular, there are seven steps to defining your own success—if you can follow these steps, you are likely to find that you can find that success for yourself.

First, you must ask yourself what success looks like to you. Figure out what it is that you want out of life and write it down for yourself. Do you want a life that is defined by being comfortable? Perhaps you want to ensure that you are happy. Maybe it is with a partner, exactly three children, a nice minivan parked in the driveway, and a nice, middle-class home that you own. This is a perfectly okay picture of success—if your dream is to have a family. It may be. Ultimately, however, your picture of success should directly reflect what you want in life.

With that picture of success in mind, it is time to make a plan. This is when you figure out exactly how you will achieve that success that you so deeply desire. This step is critical for ensuring that you are actually able to achieve your success—a plan that is not actually planned out is not likely to pan out either, and that is problematic. Make sure that your plan is as specific as possible as you do make it, as well. With a specific plan in mind, you are far more likely to achieve it than you may actually believe.

At this point, you need to make your goal happen. Do what you must and see what happens as a result. Is the other party happy with you? Do you like the results? Was it everything that you ever wanted? This is a critical point in this skill.

Finally, you must determine whether you were actually successful or not. If you were great! If not, try again in the future. You may need to make some tweaks to what you are doing, but it will be worth it when you finish your work up with ease and find that your success has, in fact, been achieved once and for all. In making sure that you never give up, you promise yourself to remain resilient and steadfast in your attempt to achieve success for yourself.

Psychology of Success and Emotional Intelligence

Remember, if you want to be successful, you want to be emotionally intelligent. This means you want to learn to begin with all of those regulation skills that have been discussed thus far. You want to learn if you can, in fact, successfully pull off those stretch goals that you have been reaching for. If you do succeed, great! If not, remember that it is not the end of the world.

Those who are emotionally intelligent tend to also be quite skilled when it comes to coping with stress and discomfort. Thanks to the fact that they are great at self-regulation, you can usually keep the stress and discomfort at bay. This means that you can actively protect yourself in ways that you did not think were possible at some points in time.

Emotionally intelligent individuals are able to cope with the stress and overwhelming feelings that come along with failure as well—when they do face that fear and discomfort, they tend to figure out how best to cope with it. The emotionally intelligent individual may make it a point, for example, to try again. This sort of resilience is critical to those who are trying to be successful. If you can be successful through making it a point to deal with failure, you are effectively learning through trial and error without ever letting someone else hurt or impact yourself negatively.

When you are faced with failure, you instead decide to learn from it. You figure out a new way to tackle the problem, and much of the time, when you do behave in such a way, you find that you are actually far more likely to get further in life. You figure out how best to take care of yourself, and that brings with it a happiness and feeling of success. Effectively, because you continued to try and were perseverant, you eventually found the solution on your own, and that is worthy of praise itself.

This means, then, if you wish to be more successful in general, you want to figure out how best to go about becoming emotionally intelligent. You want to actively become emotionally intelligent to pursue that definition of success, no matter what that definition is. If you are able to bolster your own EQ skills, you may find that you are far more likely to finally achieve that success when you reach for it.

Building Emotional Intelligence

Trying to figure out how best to build your emotional intelligence if you do not know what you are doing or where you are going is incredibly difficult. However, thanks to this book, you are getting a short guide right here. In fact, this section will provide you with several tips to help build your emotional intelligence to levels at which you will be far more effective in general.

Find Assertion

Remember, assertive is not the same as aggressive. If you can figure out how to be seen as assertive, you can ensure that people do not see you as too aggressive and, therefore, too threatening or too timid and therefore a risk of being abused into giving them free things, for example.

Learn active listening

It is critical for those who wish to be successful in having strong, active listening skills. When you find that your skillset, you commonly spend far too much time looking at yourself and how you feel instead of learning what other people are truly trying to communicate. For example, imagine that you are in a fight with your partner. If you are able to communicate clearly through the methods associated with emotional intelligence, you are far more likely to find that you are actually able to figure out the problem at the end of the day. Effectively, active listening will encourage attention and learning skills.

Developing your own motivation

One of the crucial differences between people who are successful and those who are not is primarily a matter of whether or not someone is able to put up with some negative behaviors and if you are willing to put up with it, but rather what your own motivations are. When you know what your own motivations are, you can usually figure out exactly what you need to do in order to actively and accurately what you want in life. Understanding your motivation and coming up with a goal for yourself can help immensely.

Become an optimist

Another critical skill in emotional intelligence is optimism. If you want to be optimistic, you are far more likely to succeed simply because you will have positive mindsets. Remember, mindsets are contagious, and if you think in a positive mindset, you are likely to attract more positivity to yourself as well. For this reason, you want to make it a point to always look on the bright side of things to ensure that you are actually as happy as you need to be in order to truly be successful in the first place.

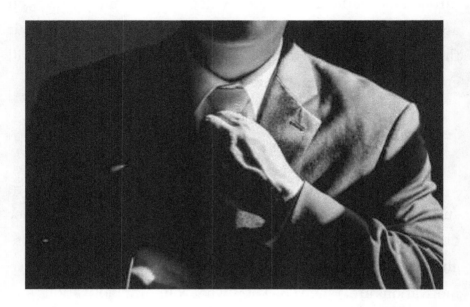

Be self-aware

If you want to be successful, you must also be self-aware. In being self-aware, you are effectively able to self-regulate when you are not happy or optimistic. Effectively, you are able to begin progressing in your work because you no longer have to worry about actively trying to project something in particular. Your ability to become self-aware is all that you need.

Learn to Empathize

Success comes primarily from within you, but most of the time, other people are still relevant to it. You need to make sure that you interact with other people as well to be as successful as possible. This means then that you have no choice but to actively try to empathize with other people. Empathy brings with it better understanding, and better understanding brings with it better relationships, and those relationships push you in the right direction toward the success that you naturally want and crave.

Develop Open Body Language

Perhaps a critical skill, if you wish to be successful at anything involving other people, you are going to want to make sure that you actively develop body language that is inviting rather than shut off from the world. This means making it a priority to emphasize smiles, keeping your body language relaxed, and more. When you do this, you find that people are far friendlier than you realized. Effectively, people all want to see you and interact with you when you are actively friendly and helping other people out.

Developing Emotional Intelligence for Leadership

When you do actively decide that emotional intelligence is right for you or that you absolutely want to be in some sort of leadership position, perhaps the best thing that you can do is push those emotional intelligence skills in order to actually ensure that you are on the right track for leadership and success.

The Positivity Challenge

Considering that perhaps one of the largest threats to your success is your own attitude, especially if that attitude is one of indifference or negativity, changing your own mindset to become positive is one of the best ways to increase your chances of success. Consider for a moment how many negative thoughts go through your mind in the course of a day. You may find that you are happy one minute, but as soon as you drop a mug that shatters, you find yourself furious and telling yourself that you are stupid. This is problematic—you should never be that negative to yourself.

When you do find yourself in a negative moment, one of the best things that you can do is ensure that you are able to actively challenging negative thoughts with positive ones. You will be tasked with providing three positive tasks to anything you word one toward negatively.

For example, imagine that you tell yourself that you are stupid. Now, you must come up with three distinct positives, and they should all be about yourself. When you do this, you are effectively shifting your own thinking, allowing yourself to think in positive manners instead of the negative ones.

Effectively, you are actively teaching yourself to figure out how best to avoid all of the negativity by drowning it in a sea of positivity. Very quickly, after several reiterations of actively having to figure out how to positively address a situation that you have had a negative thought about, you are likely to begin sort of curtailing the habit, especially if it is tied to some sort of reward for yourself.

Gratefulness Challenge

Similar to the idea of having that positive thought challenge, you must also come up with a challenge about things that you are grateful for. You think, for example, that you are not grateful enough with what you got for Christmas because you feel like the items that were bought for you were items that probably would have been better served toward the other person.

When you are attempting the gratefulness challenge, you effectively want to ensure that you are able to practice gratefulness on a regular basis. You want to make sure that you can actually recognize what you are happy to have that is not entitled to you, and you are happy to thank those who have worked so hard to give you what you have.

Perhaps one of the best ways to do a gratefulness challenge, however, is done on paper and pencil to write down what you are happy and grateful for. You may write down what you are grateful that you have food, for example, or that you are thankful for the clothing or dog food that was donated to a dog that had nothing to give. When you acknowledge out loud or on paper what you are grateful for, it can help you greatly in figuring out what to do next and where to go from there.

The Eye Contact Challenge

This does not mean that you should be actively attempting to have staring contests with everyone around you—instead, you should be actively attempting to maintain eye contact at a healthy level. You will want to be able to actively make that eye contact with other people if you ever hope to have a good chance of success.

Because so much of success depends upon other people, you need to be able to look at people in the eyes. If you are able to make eye contact, you are far more likely to be able to get that success simply because you will be better at interacting with other people. If you can do so, you will find that you are perceived to be better socially than if you were unable to make eye contact at all.

To do this challenge, you must make it a point to work up to eye contact for extended periods of time with other people. In particular, the magic number is 50% when speaking, 70% of the time when listening. This is imperative—it is the perfect amount to let the other person know that you care about what they think while also actively avoiding staring down the other person to the point that he or she feels uncomfortable. Instead, you keep eye contact somewhat causal while still quite attentive with them.

Chapter 8: Using Psychology to Fight Procrastination

And finally—you have arrived at the end of the book! Here, you will be tasked with figuring out exactly what you need to do, how to do it, and why it matters. Effectively, in this method, you will be figuring out exactly how you should approach situations of procrastination, which can be some of the most difficult to ever actually get out of simply due to the nature of the problem.

Everyone procrastinates now and then, however sometimes, it gets to a point in which it is overwhelming—it is so problematic that you are actively procrastinating that you fail to get things done by their deadlines much of the time. Slowly, bit by bit, you find that your procrastination is taking over your life and ruining it. You want to do your work, and you know that you have work to do, and yet instead, you find that you are stuck.

Within this last chapter, we will be addressing procrastination in general. We will look at what it is and what the problem with procrastination is. You will see some of the most common reasons people around you tend to procrastinate, and finally, you will be exposed to several of the methods through which you can defeat procrastination once and for all. In doing so, you may be surprised to find many of your issues relating to time management will disappear altogether.

In making these issues disappear, you may find that your stress level also declines dramatically, and with that decreased stress level, you may be better suited toward continuing to get your work done. This is good—with less procrastination comes more productivity, and that productivity is what you are looking for if you wish to be successful.

The Problem with Procrastination

Procrastination is incredibly difficult to cope with—it becomes habitual after a while, and it is only in demolishing that procrastination problem that you are ever actually able to defeat it. In defeating it, you will begin to improve your success, but until you get to that point, you are going to have to practice extreme self-control if you wish to bring that procrastination problem to a grinding halt.

First, let's look at what procrastination is. At its core, procrastination is the absence of doing what you should be at any given moment. You are actively choosing to do something contrary to what you should be, even though you know that you are making a bad choice. This means that it is nowhere near the same as laziness, which involves apathy. In this case, it is a willingness to do something entirely unrelated to what needs to get done.

Typically, people procrastinate because whatever it is that they have been tasked to do is boring, uncomfortable, or generally unpleasant in nature, and they decide that they are better off simply avoiding doing it altogether. However, all this does is cause more problems in the end. It leads to you instead trying to haphazardly rush through everything at the last minute instead of taking your time to get everything done with meticulous attention to detail as is usually expected of you.

Nevertheless, people everywhere continue to procrastinate. Even knowing that procrastination is something harmful, it is done anyway willingly. Of course, then, in response, work builds up instead of gets done. It becomes a matter of having a backlog of poorly done work instead of having your work done meticulously in advance, and that is problematic.

Why People Procrastinate

People tend to procrastinate for all sorts of reasons. Some do so because they are bored and do not want to do what they are supposed to be doing. Others do it because they would rather find something fun or enjoyable to do. Others still do it out of compulsive habit. They become so habituated to procrastination that it becomes this vicious cycle that is incredibly difficult to escape.

Consider for a moment that you have been procrastinating on that big paper for your politics class all week. You knew that it was coming up—it had been in your calendar for months, and yet, you still had not touched it. Knowing that it was due tomorrow, you looked it up this evening, only to find that you have no idea what you are doing. You choose to instead spend some time watching television instead of working on it.

A little bit later, you remind yourself that you have no choice but to get that work done if you want to actually get through it. You go to sit down at the paper, but you cannot help but feel stressed as you sit there. Soon, you are on social media instead of working, and soon after that, you find yourself constantly reading messages online.

Though you may not be aware of it, this is all because you have developed a tendency to be afraid of tests in general. You know that you usually struggle with tests, and because of that, you find that you stress out about them for a few weeks before they arrive. Of course, because you spend all of that time incredibly nervous and not studying effectively, you are nowhere near prepared on the morning of. You submit your paper and hope for the best.

In the end, you really struggled. However, that failure could actually have been a good thing. Had you been any quicker or they been any slower, you would have been able to figure out exactly how to tackle the problem sooner. However, instead, you failed and then took that failure to heart. That failure taken to heart becomes the reason that you struggle to get work done.

Effectively, getting the work done becomes stressful. When you are at work, you do not have any real leeway in your schedule. However, at home, that leeway is there—and you use it all and then some. This problem leads you to constantly be running late on everything.

However, if you were to stop and consider what was actually happening in the moment, you would realize that it was actually a cycle of anxiety. You are afraid of failure, so you struggle to begin. In struggling to begin, you run late. In running late, you fail. You then effectively solidified that particular negative thought—you *did* fail. Therefore, you must be a failure.

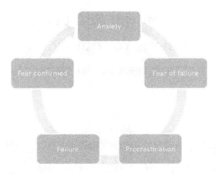

Remaining stuck in that mindset is incredibly unproductive, however, and it is in your best interest to ensure that you are able to actively figure out how best to combat that as soon as you can.

The problem, however, is that the mind is effectively hardwired to follow the negative habit of procrastination. It is designed to avoid any sort of negativity. When you are procrastinating, you are avoiding some sort of negative stimulus, and at the end of the day, you are designed to do exactly that. Effectively, you get hit with anxiety, and that anxiety sends you into fight or flight mode. You then instinctively go into flight mode, allowing for further procrastination despite the fact that it is so incredibly harmful to the individual. You struggle to actually keep up, and your stress levels then skyrocket in response and you are left disappointing those counting on you.

Defeating Procrastination with Psychology

Defeating procrastination is all about learning how to kick back those feelings of negativity in order to bring back productivity. If you can get yourself working in productivity instead of negativity, you will find that you can begin to meet those deadlines once more. You can actively get yourself working toward exactly what you needed to since you will be motivated, rather than being avoidant.

While defeating your procrastination problem may seem incredibly intimidating, it is quite doable. At the end of the day, all you need to do is figure out how best to tap into your mind to visualize exactly what you want. You need to force your mind to see that procrastinating is the enemy—despite the fact that it seems to be exactly what you want in the moment, it is actually hurting you far more than it is helping, and that can be incredibly intimidating. When you feel like you cannot benefit from procrastination any longer, you may be more willing to avoid it in the future, essentially hijacking your mind to push toward motivation as the default state once more.

As your mind accepts that motivated and achieving is the right state to be in, you will find that you are actually far more likely than ever to succeed. Your motivation is attractive to other people, and new opportunities will arise for you in the end. You will start to see long-term benefits that arise if you can just convince your mind that what you need to do more than anything else is to figure out how best to be motivated once more.

Visualize Your Future

Perhaps one of the most versatile tools that you have in your arsenal is your ability to visualize. You can visualize nearly anything—you can fantasize about something that you have always wanted, or you can fantasize about success. Ultimately, what you will be doing here is fantasizing over whatever it is that is incredibly important to you. If for you, what is important is success, you would envision that success exactly as you think it looks. Effectively, you want to show yourself exactly what it is that you want and exactly how you hope to get it. If you do this, you are likely to ensure that your mind gets a taste for what may be in store if you are able to actively push for it.

For example, imagine that you know that you have a vacation coming up. You know that you do not want to take your work on vacation, but you will have to do so if you do not take care of everything that needs to be done. Imagine for a moment how you would feel working away in your room while also watching out the window as people enjoy the beach outside without you. If you do not get that work done, that will be your future. You want to stress to yourself that in failing to meet that deadline for yourself, you are going to have no choice but to continue down that road. Remind yourself that you have plenty of time to actually meet your goals if you spend the time to get through all the work without actually procrastinating, and then encourage yourself to do exactly that. You want to make sure that you are able to actually get that work done so you can be free.

Now, imagine that same vacation if you were to spend the time to get your work done ahead of time. Think of the beach—the sand underneath your feet and the sound of the ocean lapping at the shore. Remind yourself that you would absolutely love to spend your time there instead of at home or in the hotel working. Remind yourself that the point of your vacation is to leave your work behind and to take a quick break. Tell yourself that if you want that break, you will need to work while committing that thought to memory. Burn the image of your vacation destination into your mind and summon it into your mind's eye every time you feel yourself beginning to procrastinate at all. In doing so, you will make sure that you deter yourself from procrastination every time you start to feel tempted to do so.

If done correctly, your mind will be willing to go through finishing the work as planned simply because it now feels like working on vacation is far worse than working at work when you'd rather watch another cat video. Because your mind is reminding itself that if you were to not work when it was work time, you would work more during the vacation, you will find that you are more likely to actively work and stay on schedule.

Accountability

People frequently find themselves workout buddies for the sole purpose of accountability. All things considered, working out with someone else can be quite distracting, but at the very least, it offers a level of accountability that you otherwise will not have. At that point, if you are to procrastinate, you will not only be letting yourself down—you will be letting down the other person as well. You will be making them go to the gym on their own instead of going with a friend that is going at the same time.

The idea of holding yourself accountable is incredibly powerful—humans tend to feel like they must be held accountable simply because telling other people that you have failed is generally not particularly enjoyable. If you have told other people that you were going to be doing something, you will feel the urge to ensure that you follow through simply due to the accountability.

Because people want to be seen as consistent, they tend to follow through when they voice that they are going to do something, and this is exactly why you end up doing exactly as promised when you are telling others what you are up to. Effectively, you are making sure that other people will follow up and ask you about your work, or you are making sure that someone else will be actively looking for you wherever you are supposed to be. If you are supposed to be at the gym working out, you will have someone looking for you and expecting you to spot them.

It is generally much harder for people to be willing to let down others than to let down themselves, and this is why it is so important to set up that accountability—people will follow along simply because they want to avoid letting down others who may be following or paying attention to what they are doing.

Bribes

Finally, one last way that you can keep yourself motivated is through the use of bribes. In psychology, this method is known as positive reinforcement—you actively reward good, positive behavior. Because of this, you can use bribes to effectively get people to stay on track with their work. You will do this if you want to ensure that everyone is doing what they said that they would do and what they need to do.

Imagine that you have a 30-page file to get through at work. You may feel like that is far too much and continue to push it off simply because you do not want to work on it. As you do this, you find that it is getting pushed off simply because you do not want to do it in the first place. With that in mind, you instead make it a point to actively bribe yourself to get through the work.

You decide that, after every 5 files you get through, you are free to spend 30 minutes playing a video game that you have been dying to play. Once all of the files are done, you tell yourself, you will buy yourself that new game that you have been dying to get your hands on as well. Effectively, you layer on so much positivity to what you need to get done that suddenly, getting through everything is a breeze. You may find that those files are finished up far quicker than they otherwise would have been, freeing you up and allowing you to move on with your life without worrying about procrastination continuing to eat away at your time and energy.

Eventually, you find that all files are done, and you feel quite accomplished and proud. This alone is a positive reinforcement, but when you add in the idea of actually getting a new game as well, you have doubly reinforced that new action. You are beginning to see procrastinating as less of an attempt to avoid work and more of an attempt to be lazy, and little by little, you find that you get better about actively finishing up all of your work without complaint. Eventually, you are even able to develop that internal motivation that comes from yourself. So long as you learn how to tap into that motivation, you will find that everything else comes naturally.

As with the vast majority of difficult tasks and difficult habits to break, the hardest part is the beginning. As soon as you get started and get past that first hurdle, it does get easier. It becomes easier and easier to find that intrinsic motivation within yourself to help you, and you are far more likely to succeed. All you need to do is get past that first push once and for all. Remember, you can do it. You just need to set your mind to it.

Conclusion

Congratulations! You have arrived at the end of *Introducing Psychology!* At this point, you should have a pretty solid idea on the foundation of psychology, what it entails, and how you should approach it. It is of the utmost hope that you have found this book to be at least as informative as it was intended to be. The book was designed to teach about psychology as much as possible within a short period of time, and while it is not a complete textbook the way something for psychology 101 in college may be, it is still jam-packed with some of the basic principles of psychology, such as what emotions are, what causes them, why they exist, and more.

As you read this book, it is with hope that you begin to put some of the work discussed into practice. Make it a point to remind yourself how happy you are with your partner to help build your relationship. Spend time talking to coworkers about your goals, so you work harder toward them simply because you expect the subject to be brought up over and over again when your coworkers get curious. Remind yourself that emotions are so incredibly important to understand and why they matter.

From here, you have several choices in where to go. You could make it a point to look into some of the most popular self-help fields of psychology. These are most commonly cognitive behavioral therapy, dark psychology, subliminal psychology, and emotional intelligence. Any one of these subjects would provide plenty of information about the mind, as well as provide you with more on it all.

Remember, this book is meant to cover plenty of different topics—if you wish, you can go more in-depth for literally any of them. You can choose to learn more about empathy or how to interact with other people. No matter what you choose, however, you know that you are making a good choice simply because you are actively learning. Active learning is critical if you wish to be successful.

As this book draws to a close once and for all, remember that you are capable. Whether to regulate your emotions, tackle your anger, or even to help you become successful in relationships and with other people in general, this book had help to offer you. This book wanted to provide you with all of the basic information necessary to think about the topics included.

Finally, if you have enjoyed this book at all, please consider leaving a review with your honest opinion. It is always greatly appreciated to have the opinion of a reader written out, and it would be an honor to have yours as well. Thank you so much for joining me on this journey through the mind from beginning to end. Hopefully, you found it insightful, enjoyable, and overall, quite pleasant. Good luck on your journey. If you set your mind to it, you will be able to do just about anything. Remember, you hold the power of your mind—all you need to do is learn how to tap into it once and for all. If you do so, you will be able to actively engage with your mind in the most productive manner possible.

CPSIA information can be obtained
at www.ICGtesting.com
Printed in the USA
BVHW070145301020
592123BV00013B/1711